NEW 2018

by ARGO
BROTHERS

COMMON CORE
MATH

GRADE 2

PART II: FREE RESPONSE

Visit **www.argoprep.com** to get
FREE access to our online platform.

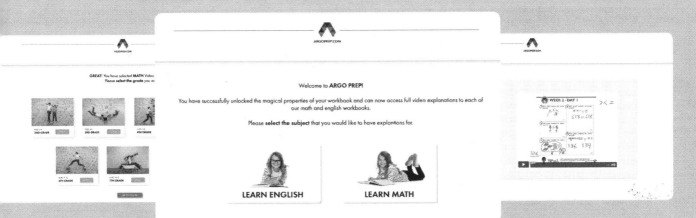

1000+ Minutes of Video Explanations and more!

Authors: Luann Voza, Ed.D.
Anayet Chowdhury
Eduard Suleyman
Vladislav Suleyman

Design: Vladislav Suleyman

At Argo Brothers, we are dedicated to providing quality and effective supplemental practice for your child. We would love to hear your honest feedback and **review** of our workbooks on **Amazon**.

Argo Brothers is one of the leading providers of supplemental educational products and services. We offer affordable and effective test prep solutions to educators, parents and students. Learning should be fun and easy! For that reason, most of our workbooks come with detailed video answer explanations taught by one of our fabulous instructors. Our goal is to make your life easier, so let us know how we can help you by e-mailing us at **info@argobrothers.com**.

OTHER BOOKS BY ARGO BROTHERS

Here are some other test prep workbooks by Argo Brothers you may be interested in. All of our workbooks come equipped with detailed video explanations to make your learning experience a breeze! Subscribe to our mailing list at www.argobrothers.com to receive custom updates about your education.

GRADE 2

GRADE 3

GRADE 4

GRADE 5

GRADE 6
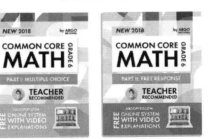

GRADE 7

GRADE 4

GRADE 5

TABLE OF CONTENTS

HOW TO USE THE BOOK

This workbook is designed to give lots of practice with the math Common Core State Standards (CCSS). By practicing and mastering this entire workbook, your child will become very familiar and comfortable with the state math exam. If you are a teacher using this workbook for your student's, you will notice each question is labeled with the specific standard so you can easily assign your students problems in the workbook. This workbook takes the CCSS and divides them up among 20 weeks. By working on these problems on a daily basis, students will be able to (1) find any deficiencies in their understanding and/or practice of math and (2) have small successes each day that will build proficiency and confidence in their abilities.

You can find detailed video explanations to each problem in the book by visiting: **www.argoprep.com**

We strongly recommend watching the videos as it will reinforce the fundamental concepts. Please note, scrap paper may be necessary while using this workbook so that the student has sufficient space to show their work.

For a detailed overview of the Common Core State Standards for 2nd grade, please visit: www.corestandards.org/Math/Content/2/introduction/

For more practice with 2nd Grade Math, be sure to check out our other book,
Argo Brothers Math Workbook Grade 2: Multiple Choice

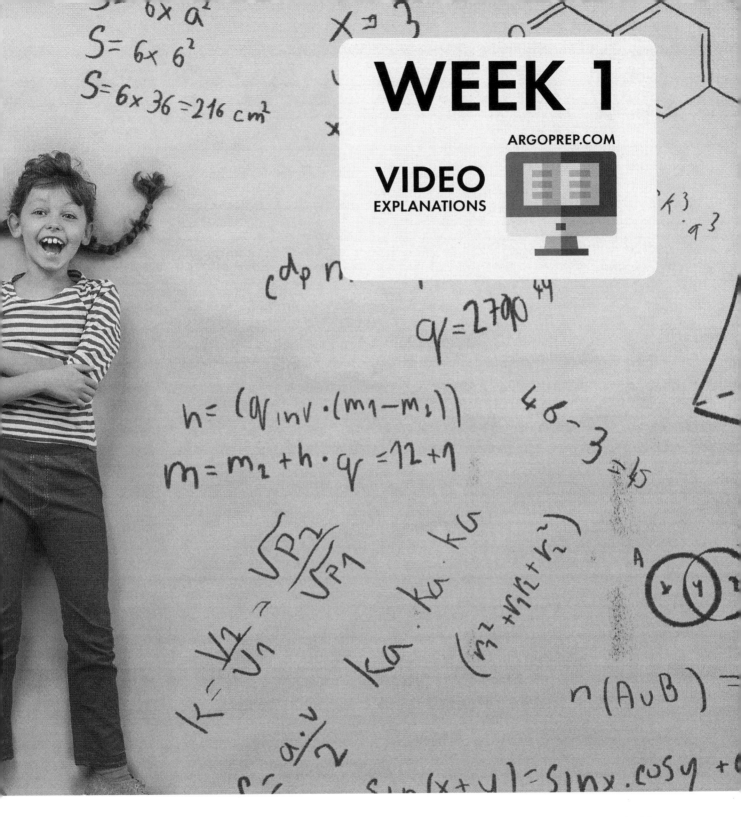

This week we are reading and writing numbers using standard form, word form and expanded form. The numbers will be up to 3 digit numbers.

You can find detailed video explanations to each problem in the book by visiting:
ArgoPrep.com

ARGOPREP.COM

1. What number is shown using the base ten pieces? **(Look at Diagram 1 below).**

_____

2.NBT.3

2. How many hundreds are in the number 528?

_____

2.NBT.1

3. In the number 2<u>3</u>7, the digit 3 is in what place?

_____

2.NBT.1

4. What number has 6 tens, 9 ones and 2 hundreds?

_____

2.NBT.1

5. What is the value of the digit 2 in the number 124?

_____

2.NBT.1

6. In the number 919, what two places have the same digit?

_____

2.NBT.3

We use the **digits** 0-1-2-3-4-5-6-7-8-9 to form numbers. The **value** of the digit is based on the **place** that the digit is in

For example: 2 in the _ones_ place has a value of _2_
2 in the _tens_ place has a value of _20_
2 in the _hundreds_ place has a value of _200_

TIP of the DAY

Hundreds Place   Tens Place   Ones Place

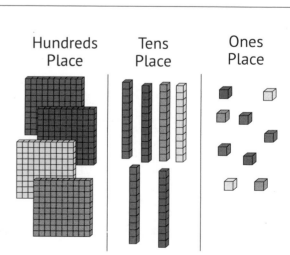

8

1. How many tens are in the number 100?

_____

2.NBT.1a

2. What number has 5 hundreds and 6 tens?

_____

2.NBT.1

3. What number has 8 ones and 1 ten?

_____

2.NBT.1

4. How many hundreds, tens and ones are in the number 500?

_____

2.NBT.1b

5. In the number 902, what place has a value of 0?

_____

2.NBT.1

Hundreds	Tens	Ones
		☐ ☐
		☐ ☐
		☐ ☐
		☐ ☐
		☐ ☐

6. The model above shows how many tens or how many ones?

_____

2.NBT.1a

When we have a total of 10 of one place, it is equal to 1 of the place to the left.

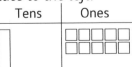

Tens | Ones

10 ones = 1 ten

When we have no value in a place, we use the digit 0.
105 = 1 hundred, 0 tens, 5 ones

TIP of the **DAY**

1. What is the written form of the number 423?

_____

2.NBT.3

2. What is the expanded form of 4 hundreds and 7 tens?

_____

2.NBT.1
2.NBT.3

3. What is the standard form of the number six hundred twenty-seven?

_____

2.NBT.3

4. What is the written form of 800 + 30 + 2?

_____

2.NBT.3

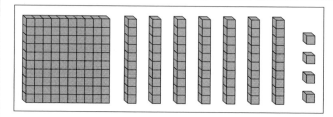

5. What is the expanded form of the number shown above?

_____

2.NBT.3

Numbers can be written in standard form, written form and expanded form.

Standard Form	Written Form	Expanded Form
123	One hundred twenty-three	100 + 20 + 3

ARGOPREP.COM

1. Start at 500 and skip-count by 100. What would be the first 5 numbers?

_____

2.NBT.2

2. Start at 50 and skip-count by 5. What would be the first 5 numbers?

_____

2.NBT.2

3. Ana's number pattern is shown: 280, 290, 300, 310, 320

Ana is skip-counting by what number in her number pattern?

_____

2.NBT.2

4. Start at the number shown by the base ten pieces and skip-count by 5.

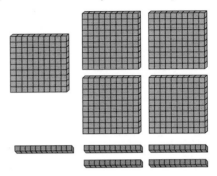

What would be the first 5 numbers?

_____

2.NBT.2
2.NBT.3

5. Start at the number shown: 3 hundreds, 0 tens, 0 ones

Skip count by 100. What would be the first 5 numbers?

_____

2.NBT.1
2.NBT.2

6. A number pattern is shown: 70 _____ 90 _____ _____ 120

What are the missing numbers?

2.NBT.2

When skip-counting by a given number, just keep adding the same number. Example: Counting by 10s from the number 30. 30, 40, 50, 60...

TIP of the DAY

1. What number sentence is shown by the model?

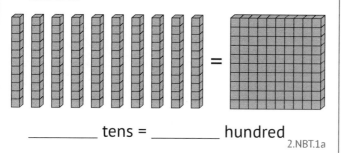

_____ tens = _____ hundred

2.NBT.1a

4. What is the expanded form of the number shown by the model?

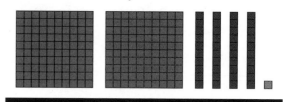

_____

2.NBT.3

2. What is the written form of the number shown in the chart?

H	T	O
1	7	0

_____

2.NBT.3

5. Max made the number pattern shown:
390 _____ 410 420 430

What number did Max skip-counted by and what is the missing number?

_____

2.NBT.2

3. What is the standard form of the number shown?

6 tens 0 hundreds 7 ones

_____

2.NBT.1
2.NBT.3

6. What is another way to write the number 890?

_____ hundreds _____ tens _____ ones

2.NBT.1

DAY 6
CHALLENGE QUESTION

Ella wrote a number. She used the following clues:
• There is a 8 in the tens place
• There is a 3 in the hundreds place
• There is a 0 in the number
What is the standard form, written form and expanded form of Ella's number?

2.NBT.1
2.NBT.3

12

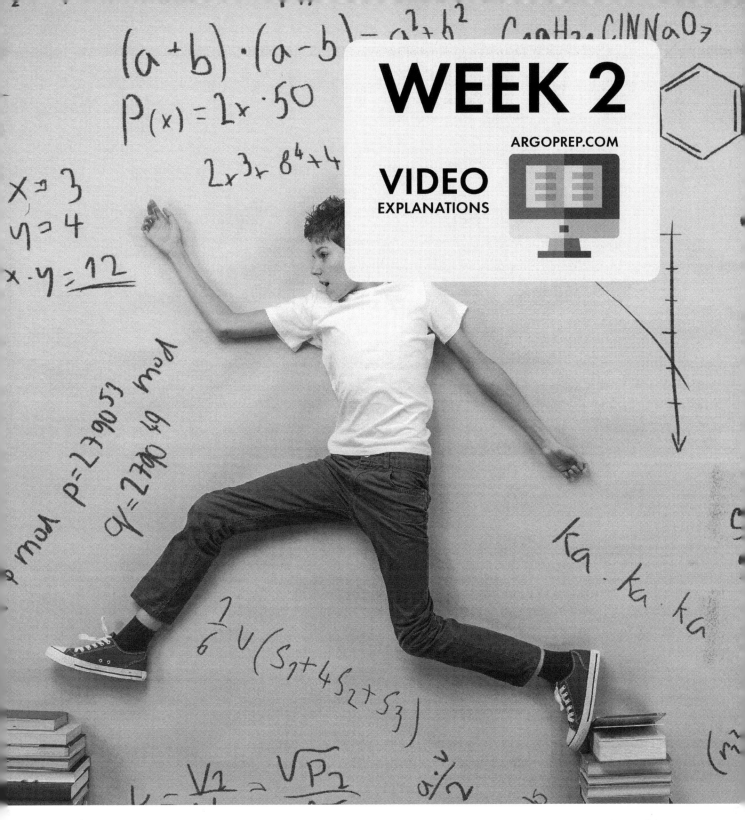

This week we are comparing numbers to find which is greater or less than another number. The numbers will be up to 3 digit numbers.

You can find detailed video explanations to each problem in the book by visiting: ArgoPrep.com

ARGOPREP.COM

1. What symbol completes the number sentence?

882 _____ 979

2.NBT.4

2. What symbol completes the number sentence?

424 _____ 432

2.NBT.4

3. What symbol completes the number sentence?

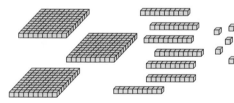

? 375

2.NBT.3
2.NBT.4

4. What symbol completes the number sentence?

600 + 10 + 8 _____ 618

2.NBT.3
2.NBT.4

5. What symbol completes the number sentence?

One hundred thirty-six _____ 100 + 4 + 30

2.NBT.3
2.NBT.4

TIP of the DAY

When comparing/ordering numbers in two different forms (standard, word, expanded) re-write them both in standard form before comparing them.

1. What symbol completes the number sentence?

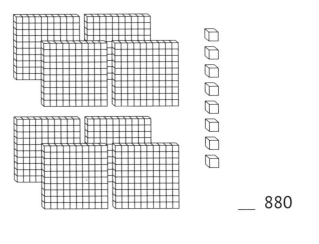

__ 880

2.NBT.3
2.NBT.4

2. What symbol completes the number sentence?

4 hundreds, 5 tens, 0 ones _____ 454

2.NBT.3
2.NBT.4

3. Which number completes the number sentence?

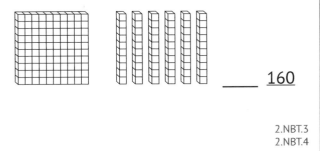

_____ 160

2.NBT.3
2.NBT.4

4. What symbol completes the number sentence?

Five hundred seven _____ 500 + 60

2.NBT.3
2.NBT.4

5. What symbol completes the number sentence?

800 + 2 + 80 _____ 881

2.NBT.3
2.NBT.4

When comparing two numbers with the same number of digits, the digit in the largest place should be compared first. If those digits are the same, look to the digit to the right. If they are still the same, continue looking to the next digit to the right to compare.

ARGOPREP.COM

1. What digit will make the number sentence correct?

$$836 < 8\_\_2$$

2.NBT.4

2. What digit will make the number sentence correct?

6 tens, 5 hundreds and 4 ones < __65

2.NBT.1
2.NBT.4

3. What digit will make the number sentence correct?

Four hundred seventy > 4 hundreds _____ tens 7 ones

2.NBT.1
2.NBT.4

4. The table shows the number of shirts in 4 different colors at a store.

Shirt Color	Red	Blue	Green	Yellow
Number of Shirts	104	121	112	103

What color was the greatest number of shirts sold?

_____

2.NBT.4

5. The table shows the number of children in grades 1, 2 and 3.

Grade	1	2	3
Number of Children	179	161	?

The number of children in grade 1 > The number of children in grade 3

The number of children in grade 3 > The number of children in grade 2

What could be the number of children in grade 3?

_____

2.NBT.4

TIP of the DAY

When comparing numbers with missing digits, place the answer choices in the blanks to find the answer.

1. What symbol completes the number sentence?

5 hundreds and 11 tens _____ 610

2.NBT.1
2.NBT.4

2. What symbol completes the number sentence?

7 hundreds, 2 tens, 14 ones _____ 724

2.NBT.1
2.NBT.4

3. What digit makes the number sentence correct?

5 hundreds, 7 tens, 16 ones = 5_2_6

_____

2.NBT.1
2.NBT.4

4. What symbol completes the number sentence?

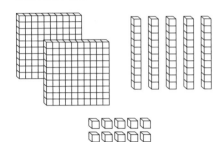

_____?_____ 265

2.NBT.3
2.NBT.4

5. What symbol completes the number sentence?

713 _____ 6 hundreds 11 tens 4 ones

2.NBT.1
2.NBT.4

6. What symbol completes the number sentence?

__?__ 8 hundreds 4 tens 12 ones

2.NBT.3
2.NBT 4

Numbers can be written in more than one way.
For example: 82 can be written as 8 tens and 2 ones or 7 tens and 12 ones.
340 can be written as 3 hundreds and 4 tens or 2 hundreds and 14 tens.
When comparing numbers, be sure to use the standard form of both numbers.

TIP of the **DAY**

1. What symbol completes the number sentence?

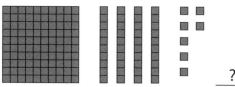

_____? 147

2.NBT.3
2.NBT.4

2. What symbol completes the number sentence?

6 hundreds 4 tens 11 ones _____ 641

2.NBT.1
2.NBT.4

3. What digit could complete the number sentence?

Nine hundred seventy-two >
9 hundreds _____ tens 4 ones

_____

2.NBT.1
2.NBT.4

4. The number of flowers in the garden is less than 415 and greater than 409.

What could be the number of flowers in the garden?

_____

2.NBT.4

5. What symbol completes the number sentence?

4 hundreds 11 tens _____ 411

2.NBT.1
2.NBT.4

6. What symbol completes the number sentence?

3 hundreds 5 ones 1 ten _____ 351

2.NBT.1
2.NBT.4

DAY 6
CHALLENGE QUESTION

Part A: Find the mystery number using the clues:
There are 4 hundreds, There are 12 tens, There are 12 ones
Mystery Number: _____ _____ _____
Part B: Compare the mystery number to the number shown by drawing the correct symbol:
Mystery Number _____ 422

2.NBT.1

WEEK 3

ARGOPREP.COM

VIDEO EXPLANATIONS

This week we are adding single digit numbers. The numbers will be up to 9 + 9.

You can find detailed video explanations to each problem in the book by visiting:
ArgoPrep.com

1. What number completes the number sentence?

$$5 + 4 = ?$$

_____

2.OA.2

2. What is the sum of 8 and 5?

_____

2.OA.2

3. What number sentence is shown on the number line?

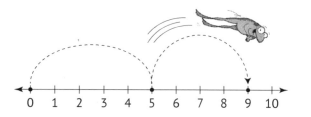

_____

2.OA.2

4. The model shows what number sentence?

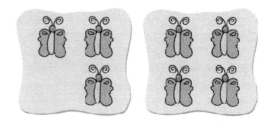

_____

2.OA.2

5. What is the sum of 7 and 0?

_____

2.OA.2

6. The number 11 is the sum for the number pair 4 + what number?

_____

2.OA.2

The answer to an addition problem is called the "sum".
For example, the sum of 3 + 2 is 5. 3 + 2 = 5

ARGOPREP.COM

1. What number completes the number sentence?

$$8 + 3 = ?$$

_____

2.OA.2

2. What number sentence is shown on the number line?

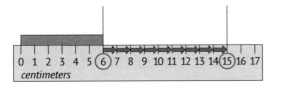

_____

2.OA.2

3. What pair of the same numbers, has a sum of 10?

_____ and _____

2.OA.2

4. The model below shows what number sentence?

6	2

_____ and _____

2.OA.2

5. What number completes the number sentence?

$$7 + 5 = ?$$

2.OA.2

6. What is the sum of $9 + 3$?

_____

2.OA.2

When adding two numbers, you can change the order and still get the same answer. For example, 4 + 1 = 1 + 4.

1. The model shows what number sentence?

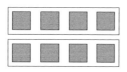

_____

2.OA.4

2. What number sentence can be solved from the model?

_____

2.OA.1
2.OA.4

3. The model shows what number sentence?

_____

2.OA.4

4. What number pair has a sum of 13 and uses a double + 1 to solve?

_____

2.OA.1

5. What number pair has a sum of 16 and uses a double to solve?

_____

2.OA.2

6. What number is the sum of 10 and 10?

_____

2.OA.2

TIP of the **DAY**

Practice your doubles like 5+5 and 6+6. Then practice adding 1 on to a double to find the sum. For example: 5 = 5 = 10 and 5 + 6 = 11 which is 10 + 1 more.

1. What number completes the number sentence?

$$8 + 4 = ?$$

_____

2.OA.2

2. What is another way to add 8 + 3 using the number 10?

_____

2.OA.2

3. What pair of number sentences does the model show?

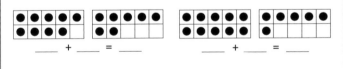

_____ + _____ = _____   _____ + _____ = _____

_____

2.OA.2

4. What pair of number sentences have the sum of 15?

_____

2.OA.2

5. What is the sum of 9 and 5?

_____

2.OA.2

6. Which number completes the number sentence?

$$7 + 5 = ?$$

_____

2.OA.2

When adding two numbers, count from the larger number up to 10, then add on the rest of the smaller number. For some, it is easier to add from 10.
For example, 9 + 3 = 10 + 2 = 12.

9 + 3 = 12   10 + 2 = 12

TIP of the **DAY**

1. What number sentence does the model show?

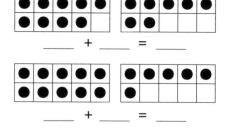

_____

2.OA.2
2.OA.4

2. What is the sum of 7 and 9?

_____

2.OA.2

3. What 2 number sentences both have a sum of 10?

_____

2.OA.2

4. What number sentence could use a double to find the sum?

_____

2.OA.2

5. What pair of number sentences shows the order changed but the sum is the same?

_____

2.OA.2

6. What pair of number sentences are shown in the model?

_____ + _____ = _____

_____ + _____ = _____

_____

2.OA.2

DAY 6
CHALLENGE QUESTION

What are 3 number sentences that have a sum of 14? Choose from the numbers 5-9. What do you notice?

2.OA.2

This week we are subtracting single digit numbers. The numbers will be up to 18 - 9.

You can find detailed video explanations to each problem in the book by visiting:
ArgoPrep.com

ARGOPREP.COM

1. What number completes the number sentence:

$$11 - 6 = ?$$

_____

2.OA.2

2. What number is the difference of 10 and 4?

_____

2.OA.2

3. What number sentence is related to the number sentence 8 + 7 = ?

_____

2.OA.2

4. What number completes the number sentence 9 − ? = 2

_____

2.OA.2

5. What number completes the number sentence?

$$13 - 6 = ?$$

_____

2.OA.2

6. What subtraction sentence is related to 9 + 9 = ?

_____

2.OA.2

TIP of the DAY

*Subtraction is related to addition. For example, 5 + 2 = 7, 7 − 5 = 2 and 7 − 2 = 5. The same three numbers are in all of the number sentences. The answer to a subtraction problem is called the **difference**.*

ARGOPREP.COM

---

1. What number completes the number sentence?

$$4 + ? = 13$$

_____

2.OA.2

---

4. What subtraction sentence is shown on the model?

3	?
7	

_____

2.OA.2

---

2. What number sentence could be used to find the answer to $9 + ? = 17$

_____

2.OA.2

---

5. What number completes the number sentence?

$$5 + ? = 13$$

_____

2.OA.2

---

3. What number shows the difference of 15 and 9?

_____

2.OA.2

---

6. What number completes the number sentence?

$$14 - 7 = ?$$

_____

2.OA.2

When finding the missing number in an addition problem, think of using a bar model to find the answer.

Whole ?

8	3

Part   Part

Add to find the whole 8 + 3 = 11

Whole 11

8	?

Part   Part

Substract to find the part 11 – 8 = 3

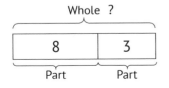

ARGOPREP.COM

1. The number line shows what number sentence?

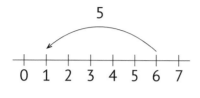

5

0 1 2 3 4 5 6 7

_____

2.OA.2

2. What number is 6 more than 8?

_____

2.OA.2

3. What number sentence does the number line show?

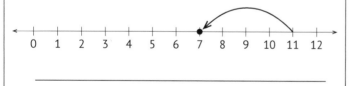

0 1 2 3 4 5 6 7 8 9 10 11 12

_____

2.OA.2

4. Use the number line to complete the statement.

0 1 2 3 4 5 6 7 8 9 10

The number _____ is _____ more than _____.

2.OA.2

Use the number line to answer questions #5 and 6.

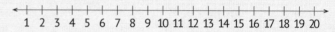

1 2 3 4 5 6 7 8 9 10 11 12 13 14 15 16 17 18 19 20

5. What number is 8 more than 9?

_____

2.OA.2

6. Two numbers have a difference of 9. One is 7. What is the other?

_____

2.OA.2

Subtracting numbers is also finding how far away two numbers are on a number line. We can also count up or back to find how much more or how much less numbers are from each other using the number line.

TIP of the **DAY**

$14 - 6 = 8$

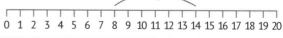

0 1 2 3 4 5 6 7 8 9 10 11 12 13 14 15 16 17 18 19 20

When comparing the numbers 14 and 8 we see that they are 6 numbers apart on the number line. When we count back we see that 8 is 6 spaces less than 14 and when we count up we see that 14 is 6 spaces more than 8.

WEEK 4 · DAY 4

ARGOPREP.COM

1. What number sentence does the array show?

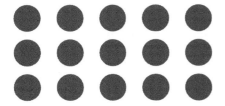

_____

2.OA.4

2. What number sentence does the array show?

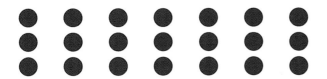

_____

2.OA.4

3. What number sentence does the array show?

_____

2.OA.4

4. What number sentence does this number line show?

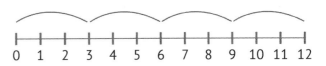

_____

2.OA.2

5. What number sentence, using the number 4, could have an array to show the sum of 16?

_____

2.OA.2

We can use arrays and number lines to show addition that is repeated (done more than one time). For example the addition sentence 4 + 4 + 4 = ? can be shown using the array.

4 + 4 = 8 and 8 + 4 = 12 so 4 + 4 + 4 = 12.

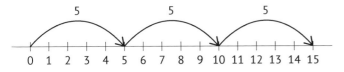

This number line shows 5 + 5 + 5 = 15

29

WEEK 4 · DAY 5
ASSESSMENT

1. What number sentence does the number line show?

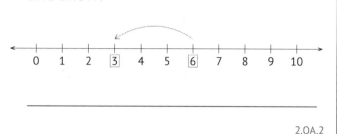

2.OA.2

2. What number sentence does the model show?

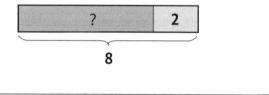

2.OA.2

3. What number sentence does the array show?

2.OA.2

4. What number is the answer to 13 − ? = 9?

2.OA.4

5. What **two** number pairs **both** have a difference of 7?

2.OA.2

DAY 6
CHALLENGE QUESTION

Which 2 numbers have a sum of 15 and a difference of 1?

2.OA.2

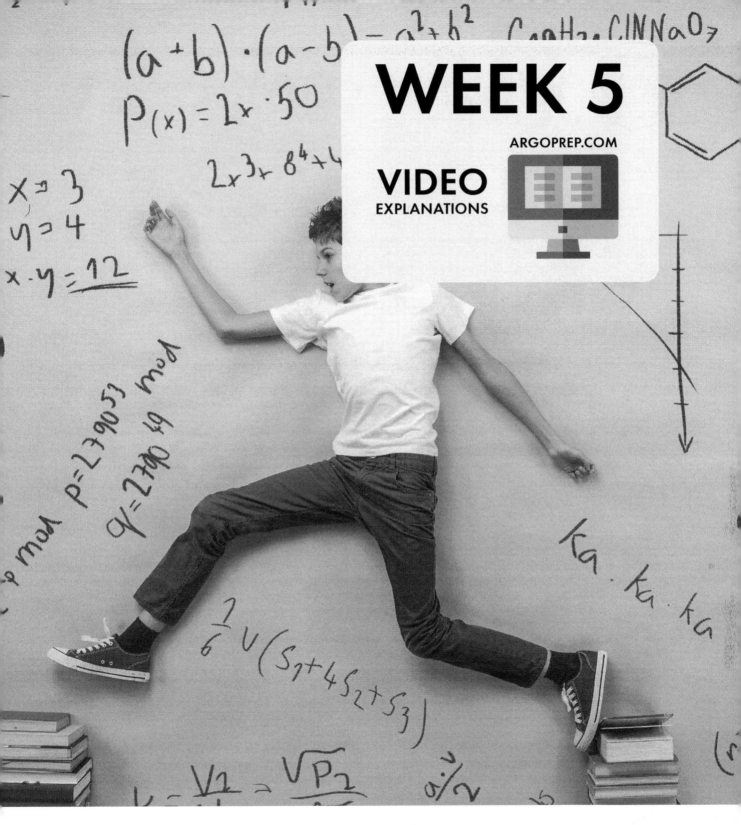

WEEK 5

This week we are telling if numbers are even or odd. The numbers will be up to 2 digit numbers.

You can find detailed video explanations to each problem in the book by visiting:
ArgoPrep.com

1. What is an even number less than 5?

_____

2.OA.3

2. What is an odd number less than 5?

_____

2.OA.3

3. Name a pair of numbers less than 10 that are both even.

_____

2.OA.3

4. Name a pair of numbers less than 10 that are both odd.

_____

2.OA.3

5. Name a pair of numbers between 10 and 15 in which one is odd and one is even.

odd: _____   even: _____

2.OA.3

Even numbers can form pairs of two and odd numbers cannot will have one left over.

2 is even   3 is odd   10 is even   7 is odd

TIP of the DAY

32

1. What are the next two even numbers after the number 10?

_____

2.OA.3

2. What are the next two odd numbers after the number 10?

_____

2.OA.3

3. What are the next 2 odd numbers after the number 15?

_____

2.OA.3

4. What are the next 2 even numbers after the number 15?

_____

2.OA.3

5. In the number set 8, 9, 10 and 11 what numbers are odd?

_____

2.OA.3

6. In the number set 9, 10, 11 and 12 what numbers are even?

_____

2.OA.3

On a number line, 1 is an odd number, 2 is an even number, and the pattern continues: odd-even-odd-even. For greater numbers, the number in the ones place tells us what is even and odd. Numbers that end with 1, 3, 5, 7, and 9 are odd and numbers that end with 2,4 6, 8, and 0 are even.

odd even odd even odd even

1 2 3 4 5 6 7 8 9 10 11 12 13 14 15 16 17 18 19 20

1. Write a number sentence with an even sum less than 5.

_____

2.OA.3

2. Write a number sentence with an odd sum less than 5.

_____

2.OA.3

3. Write a number sentence with an even sum between 5 and 10.

_____

2.OA.3

4. Write a number sentence with an even sum between 10 and 15 in which

Odd + Odd = Even

_____

2.OA.3

5. Write a number sentence with an even sum between 10 and 15 in which

Even + Even = Even

_____

2.OA.3

TIP of the DAY

When adding two of the same numbers, no matter if they are both odd or both even, the sum is even.

2	+	2	=	4		3	+	3	=	6
even	+	even	=	even		odd	+	odd	=	even

WEEK 5 · DAY 4

1. What number completes the number sentence?

$$? + 6 = 14$$

_____

2.OA.2

2. What number completes the number.2 sentence?

$$? - 7 = 6$$

_____

2.OA.2

3. What subtraction sentence could be used to find the answer?

$$? + 9 = 13$$

_____

2.OA.2

4. What addition sentence could be used to find the answer?

$$? - 4 = 7$$

_____

2.OA.2

5. What number completes the number sentence?

$$? - 7 = 1$$

_____

2.OA.2

When we don't know the first number in the number sentence, we can work backwards using the opposite of the sign.

_? + 5 = 14_	_Working backwards,_	_14 − 5 = ?_	_9 + 5 = 14_
_? − 8 = 7_	_Working backwards_	_7 + 8 = 15_	_15 − 8 = 7_

1. Using the words **Odd** and **Even,** what type of number sentence does the model show?

_____

2.OA.2

4. Write a set of numbers that has two even and one odd number.

Even: _____ _____ Odd _____

2.OA.2

2. Using the words **Odd** and **Even**, what type of number sentence does the model show?

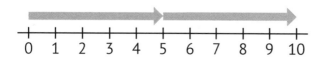

_____

2.OA.2

5. What number completes the number sentence?

$$? + 9 = 15$$

_____

2.OA.2

3. Using the words **Odd** and **Even**, what type of number sentence is shown?

$$8 + 8 = 16$$

_____

2.OA.2

6. What addition sentence could be used to find the answer?

$$? - 8 = 7$$

_____

2.OA.2

DAY 6
CHALLENGE QUESTION

A. What happens when you add an odd number and an even number? Odd + Even = ?

B. Give some examples.

C. Explain why.

2.OA.2

WEEK 6

ARGOPREP.COM

VIDEO EXPLANATIONS

This week we are using addition and subtraction to solve problems. The numbers will be up to 100.

You can find detailed video explanations to each problem in the book by visiting:
ArgoPrep.com

1. There were 50 cars parked in the front of the school. In the back there were 23 cars. How many total cars are in the front and the back?

_____

2.OA.1

2. At lunch 34 girls were sitting at the big tables. There were 20 boys sitting at the big tables. How many more girls than boys were sitting at the big tables?

_____

2.OA.1

3. The teacher has 18 red notebooks and 20 blue notebooks. How many total notebooks does the teacher have?

_____

2.OA.1

4. In the class there were 50 crayons in boxes. There were 25 crayons not in boxes. How many total crayons were in the class?

_____

2.OA.1

5. In the big box there are 52 pencils. In the small box there are 20 pencils. How many more pencils are in the big box?

_____

2.OA.1

6. A total of 72 children were outside playing. Then 20 children went into the school. How many children were still outside playing?

_____

2.OA.1

When solving word problems by adding and subtracting, making models such as bar models and number bonds are helpful.

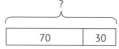

?

| 70 | 30 |

There are 70 water bottles and 30 juice bottles. How many bottles in all?

70 + 30 = 100 bottles

20	
?	11

There were 20 children on the bus. Then 11 children got off the bus. How many children are now on the bus?

20 – 11 = 9 children

21

?

27

There are 21 new pencils and 27 old pencils in the box. How many total pencils are in the box?

21 + 27 = 48 pencils

ARGOPREP.COM

1. What is the sum of 22 + 44?

_____

2.NBT.5
2.NBT.6

2. What is the sum of 38 + 41?

_____

2.NBT.5
2.NBT.6

3. What number is the difference of 54 and 23?

_____

2.NBT.5
2.NBT.6

4. What number is 20 less than 65?

_____

2.NBT.5
2.NBT.6

5. What number is 20 more than 47?

_____

2.NBT.5
2.NBT.6

6. What number completes the number sentence?

$$10 + 31 + 22?$$

_____

2.NBT.5
2.NBT.6

When adding 2 digit numbers, put the numbers neatly into columns.
Add or subtract the ones and then the tens.

```
   25          48
 + 50        − 17
 ------      ------
   75          31
```

39

1. What number completes the number sentence?

$$49 + 23 = ?$$

_____

2.NBT.5

4. What number completes the number sentence?

$$37 + 15 = ?$$

_____

2.NBT.5

2. What number is the sum of 34 and 18?

_____

2.NBT.5

5. What number is the sum of 47 and 6?

_____

2.NBT.5

3. Which number is 15 more than 67?

_____

2.NBT.5

6. What number is 24 more than 49?

_____

2.NBT.5

TIP of the **DAY**

When adding, sometimes the sum of the ones place is a 2 digit number (tens and ones), so we need to place the tens digit into the tens place.

```
 +1
  28      20 + 8
+ 17      10 + 7
  45      30 + 15 (place the 1 in the 15 above the tens place)
```

1. What number completes the number sentence?

$$63 - 25 = ?$$

_____

2.NBT.5

4. What number completes the number sentence?

$$60 - 38 = ?$$

_____

2.NBT.5

2. What number is the difference of 61 and 43?

_____

2.NBT.5

5. What number is the difference of 45 and 8?

_____

2.NBT.5

3. What number is 26 less than 74?

_____

2.NBT.5

6. What number is 23 less than 72?

_____

2.NBT.5

When subtracting, sometimes the first number needs to be renamed so that you can subtract. Be sure to check and rename the number.

	4 13		
	5̶3̶	5 tens 3 ones	4 tens 13 ones
	−16	1 ten 6 ones	1 ten 6 ones
	37		3 tens 7 ones

TIP of the DAY

1. There were 28 soccer players and 26 football players. How many total players were there?

_____

2.OA.1

2. A total of 46 cans of soda were on the table. The children drank 35 cans. How many cans of soda were now left on the table?

_____

2.OA.1

3. What number completes the number sentence?

$$31 + 22 + 12 = ?$$

_____

2.NBT.6

4. What number is the difference of 91 and 14?

_____

2.NBT.5

5. What number is 14 less than 40?

_____

2.NBT.5

6. What number is 18 more than 45?

_____

2.NBT.5

DAY 6
CHALLENGE QUESTION

A. Find two number with a sum of 65.
B. Find the difference of the same two numbers.

WEEK 7

ARGOPREP.COM

VIDEO EXPLANATIONS

This week we are adding and subtracting larger numbers from tables and models. The numbers will be up to 100.

You can find detailed video explanations to each problem in the book by visiting:
ArgoPrep.com

WEEK 7 · DAY I

ARGOPREP.COM

1. What number completes the addition problem?

$$
\begin{array}{r}
26 \\
35 \\
+\ 21 \\
\hline
\end{array}
$$

_____

2.NBT.6

2. What number is the sum of 15, 32 and 6?

_____

2.NBT.6

3. Which number completes the number sentence? 16 + 27 + 43 =?

_____

2.NBT.6

The number of children that are in the Music Club is shown in the table.

Use the table to complete questions #4-5-6

Number of Children in Art Club

Grade	Number of Boys	Number of Girls
2	15	18
3	16	17
4	21	21

4. Which shows the total number of boys in the Music Club?

_____

2.NBT.1
2.NBT.6

5. Which shows the total number of girls in the Music Club?

_____

2.NBT.1
2.NBT.6

6. Which shows the total number of children in Grades 3 and 4 in the Music Club?

_____

2.NBT.1
2.NBT.6

If you are stuck on a multiple choice math question, try to use guess and check with the given answer choices to help you solve the problem.

44

At a school, there are 4 teams that play a game each day. The table shows the teams and the number of points scored in the first 4 games.

Use the table to answer questions #1-6

Points Scored by Each Team in Each Game

Game	Red Team	Blue Team	Green Team	White Team
1	18	17	14	13
2	11	12	13	18
3	13	21	21	6
4	20	16	17	21

1. Which shows the total number of points scored by the Red team?

_____

2.OA.1
2.OA.2
2.NBT.6

2. Which shows the total number of points scored by the Blue team?

_____

2.OA.1
2.OA.2
2.NBT.6

3. Which shows the total number of points scored by the Green team?

_____

2.OA.1
2.OA.2
2.NBT.6

4. Which shows the total number of points scored by the White team?

_____

2.OA.1
2.OA.2
2.NBT.6

5. Which team scored the greatest total of points for the 4 games?

_____

2.OA.1
2.OA.2
2.NBT.6

6. Which team scored the least total of points for the 4 games?

_____

2.OA.1
2.OA.2
2.NBT.6

When using numbers in a table to add, make sure you find the right numbers to add.
Flowers in Vase

Flower Color	Red	Yellow	Pink	White
Number of Flowers	14	13	16	15

How many yellow and pink flowers are in the vase?
Only look for the numbers for yellow and pink.

$$\begin{array}{r} 13 \\ +\ 16 \\ \hline 29 \end{array}$$

pink and yellow flowers

 TIP of the DAY

The teacher has new boxes of pens, pencils, crayons and markers. The table shows the number of pens, pencils, crayons and markers that are in each new box.

Use the table to answer questions # 1-5

	Pens	Pencils	Crayons	Markers
Number in Each Box	12	28	33	17

3. Which shows the total number of pens and pencils for 1 box of pens and 2 boxes of pencils?

_____

2.OA.1
2.NBT.6

1. Which shows the total number of pens and pencils for 2 boxes of each?

_____

2.OA.1
2.NBT.6

4. Which shows the total number of crayons and markers for 1 box of crayons and 2 boxes of markers?

_____

2.OA.1
2.NBT.6

2. Which shows the total number of crayons and markers for 2 boxes of each?

_____

2.OA.1
2.NBT.6

5. Which shows the total number for 1 box of pens, pencils, crayons and markers?

_____

2.OA.1
2.NBT.6

TIP of the DAY

Day 3: Tip of the Day- When adding more than 2 numbers, look for numbers that add up to 10 and add them together first. You can add 4 + 6 = 10, then add 10 + 2 = 12.

```
  14
  12
+ 16
  42
```

ARGOPREP.COM

1. Last year there were 348 children in the school. This year there are 100 more. Which shows the number of children in the school this year?

_____

2.OA.1
2.NBT.8

2. There were 171 people at the game. Then 10 people left. How many people are now at the game?

_____

2.OA.1
2.NBT.8

3. Which number is 10 more than 467?

_____

2.OA.1
2.NBT.8

4. Which number completes the number sentence?

? + 100 = 615

_____

2.OA.1
2.NBT.8

5. Which number completes the number sentence?

? – 10 = 271

_____

2.OA.1
2.NBT.8

6. Which number completes the number sentence?

? + 10 = 729

_____

2.OA.1
2.NBT.8

When adding or subtracting 10 more, 10 less, 100 more or 100 less, make sure that you place the numbers in the right place.

		Incorrect	Correct
Add:	249 + 10	249	249
		+10	+ 10
		349	259

47

1. There are 26 clips in a small box.

There are 34 clips in a big box.

How many total clips are in 2 small boxes and 1 large box?

_____

2.OA.1

2. What number completes the number sentence?

$$52 + 23 + 9 = ?$$

_____

2.OA.1

3. Ava counted the number of birds that she saw each day for 4 days.

The table shows the day and the number of birds.

Day	1	2	3	4
Number of Birds	14	6	6	24

What is the total number of birds that Ava saw for the 4 days?

_____

2.OA.1

4. What number is 100 more than 630?

_____

2.NBT.8

5. Which number is 10 less than 783?

_____

2.NBT.8

6. Which number completes the number sentence?

$$? - 10 = 185$$

_____

2.NBT.8

DAY 6
CHALLENGE QUESTION

Last week the class brought in 83 cans.
Then they brought in 100 more.
Then they brought in 10 more.
Then they brought in 100 more.
Now how many cans are there in all?

WEEK 8

ARGOPREP.COM

VIDEO EXPLANATIONS

This week we are using what we know about place value to add and subtract large numbers. The numbers will be up to 1,000.

You can find detailed video explanations to each problem in the book by visiting:
ArgoPrep.com

1. What number completes the number sentence?

$$350 + 23 = ?$$

_____

2.NBT.7

2. What number completes the number sentence?

$$469 - 31 = ?$$

_____

2.NBT.7

3. What number is the sum of 503 + 315?

_____

2.NBT.7

4. What number is the difference of 548 and 220?

_____

2.NBT.7

5. What number completes the number sentence?

$$? + 230 = 474$$

_____

2.NBT.7

6. What number completes the number sentence?

$$? - 204 = 304$$

_____

2.NBT.7

TIP of the **DAY**

When adding 3 digit numbers, make sure you line up the numbers in the right place.

$123 + 45 = ?$

	Incorrect	Correct
	123	123
	+45	+ 45
	573	168

WEEK 8 · DAY 2

ARGOPREP.COM

---

1. What number is the sum of 273 and 162?

$$
\begin{array}{llll}
& 2 \text{ hundreds} & 7 \text{ tens} & 3 \text{ ones} \\
+ & 1 \text{ hundred} & 6 \text{ tens} & 2 \text{ ones}
\end{array}
$$

_____

2.NBT.7

---

3. What number sentence does the model show?

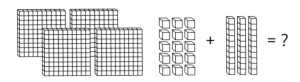

_____

2.NBT.7

---

2. The model can be used to find what sum?

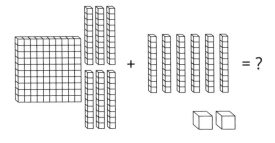

_____

2.NBT.7

---

4. The chart can be used to find what sum?

$$
\begin{array}{llll}
& 6 \text{ hundreds} & 8 \text{ tens} & 3 \text{ ones} \\
+ & 1 \text{ hundreds} & 3 \text{ tens} & 2 \text{ ones}
\end{array}
$$

_____

2.NBT.7

---

5. The model can be used to find what sum?

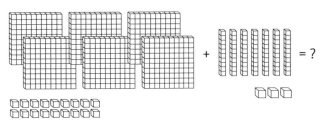

_____

2.NBT.7

Use place value charts or models to add when you need to regroup to the next place.

644	6 hundreds	4 tens	4 ones
+ 172	1 hundred	7 tens	2 ones
816	7 hundreds	11 tens	6 ones or
	8 hundreds	1 ten	6 ones

51

1. What number completes the number sentence 430 – 260?

    4 hundreds 3 tens   or   3 hundreds 13 tens
 – 2 hundreds 6 tens   –   2 hundreds   6 tens

_____

2.NBT.7

2. The model can be used for what number sentence?

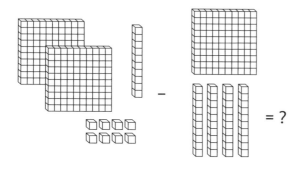

= ?

_____

2.NBT.7

3. What number completes the number sentence 805 – 415?

  8 hundreds 0 tens 5 ones   or 7 hundreds 10 tens 5 ones
 – 4 hundreds 1 ten   5 ones   –   4 hundreds   1 ten   5 ones

_____

2.NBT.7

4. The model can be used to find what difference?

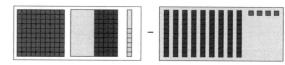

–   = ?

_____

2.NBT.7

5. What number completes the number sentence?

  2 hundreds 5 tens 4 ones = 2 hundreds _?_ tens __?_ ones
 – 1 hundred   3 tens 6 ones – 1 hundred   3 tens 6 ones

_____

2.NBT.7

TIP of the DAY

Use charts or models when you need to regroup for subtraction.
  613 6 hundreds 1 ten   3 ones or 5 hundreds 11 tens 3 ones
– 382 3 hundreds 8 tens 2 ones   3 hundreds   8 tens 2 ones
  231   2 hundreds   3 tens 1 one

Use the model for questions #1 and #2.

First Number   Second Number

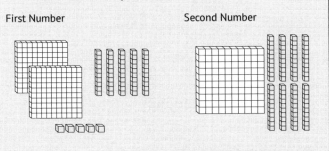

1. What number is the sum of the first and second number?

_____

2.NBT.7

2. What number is the difference of the first and second number?

_____

2.NBT.7

Use the model for questions #3 and #4.

Hundreds	Tens	Ones
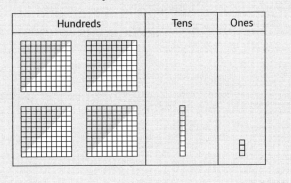		

3. What is the sum of the number in the model and 341?

_____

2.NBT.7

4. What is the difference of the number in the model and 341?

_____

2.NBT.7

Use the model for questions #5 and #6.

First Number

Second Number

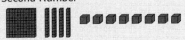

5. What is the sum of the first number and the second number?

_____

2.NBT.7

6. What is the difference of the first number and the second number?

_____

2.NBT.7

Be sure to check the sign to determine if you will be adding, finding the sum, or subtracting, finding the difference.

53

1. What number completes the number sentence?

$$610 + 308 = ?$$

_____

2.NBT.7

2. What number completes the number sentence?

$$548 - 34 = ?$$

_____

2.NBT.7

3. What number is the sum of 349 + 214?

3 hundreds 4 tens 9 ones

+ 2 hundreds 1 ten 4 ones
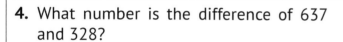

_____

2.NBT.7

4. What number is the difference of 637 and 328?

6 hundreds 3 tens 7 ones or 6 hundreds 2 tens 17 ones
– 3 hundreds 2 tens 8 ones – 3 hundreds 2 tens 8 ones

_____

2.NBT.7

Use the model for questions #5 and #6.

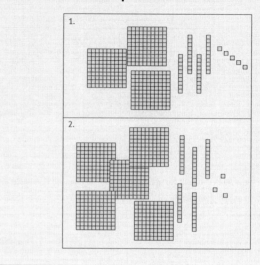

5. Which shows the sum of the first number and the second number?

_____

2.NBT.7

6. Which shows the difference of the first number and the second number?

_____

2.NBT.7

DAY 6
CHALLENGE
QUESTION

A. Find the sum of 123 and 456
B. Find the difference of 789 and 456.

WEEK 9

ARGOPREP.COM

VIDEO EXPLANATIONS

This week we are finding different ways to add and subtract numbers. Numbers will use base ten models and place value charts.

You can find detailed video explanations to each problem in the book by visiting:
ArgoPrep.com

1. What number completes the number sentence?

$$5 + 7 = 10 + ?$$

_____

1.OA.7
2.OA.2

4. What number completes the number sentence?

$$6 + 8 = 9 + ?$$

_____

1.OA.7
2.OA.2

2. What number completes the number sentence?

$$9 + 9 = 10 + ?$$

_____

1.OA.7
2.OA.2

5. What number completes the number sentence?

$$6 + 8 = 12 + ?$$

_____

1.OA.7
2.OA.2

3. What number completes the number sentence?

$$7 + 8 = 10 + ?$$

_____

1.OA.7
2.OA.2

6. What number completes the number sentence?

$$7 + 9 = 8 + ?$$

_____

1.OA.7
2.OA.2

TIP of the **DAY**

When finding the answer for longer number sentences, find the answer on one side of the equal sign first.
Which number completes the number sentence?

$$3 + 9 = 10 + ?$$

Solve $3 + 9 = 12$ $12 = 10 + ?$ _Answer: 2_

56

ARGOPREP.COM

1. What number completes the number sentence?

$$8 + 5 = 18 - ?$$

_____

1.OA.7
2.OA.2

4. What number completes the number sentence?

$$9 + 8 = 24 - ?$$

_____

1.OA.7
2.OA.1

2. What number completes the number sentence?

$$6 + 5 = 19 - ?$$

_____

1.OA.7
2.OA.2

5. What number completes the number sentence?

$$9 + 7 = ? - 2$$

_____

1.OA.7
2.OA.1

3. What number completes the number sentence?

$$5 + 9 = 16 - ?$$

_____

1.OA.7
2.OA.2

6. What number completes the number sentence?

$$8 + 8 = ? - 5$$

_____

1.OA.7
2.OA.1

Check the signs in the number sentence when finding the answer.

$$5 + 5 = 14 - ?$$

First, add the left side $5 + 5 = 10$ $10 = 14 - ?$
Now we will subtract to find what equals 10. $14 - 4 = 10.$ $? = 4$

1. What number completes the number sentence?

$$20 + 13 = ? + 10$$

_____

2.OA.1

2. What number completes the number sentence?

$$30 + 7 = 50 – ?$$

_____

2.OA.1

3. What number completes the number sentence?

$$43 + 10 = 20 + ?$$

_____

2.OA.1

4. What number completes the number sentence?

$$62 + 20 = 85 – ?$$

_____

2.OA.1

5. What number completes the number sentence?

$$85 – 30 = 25 + ?$$

_____

2.OA.1

6. What number completes the number sentence?

$$25 + 25 = 85 – ?$$

_____

2.OA.1

TIP of the **DAY**

When you find the answer, do the problem again with your answer to see if it is correct.

$4 + 10 = 30 – ?$

$4 + 10 = 14$ $30 – ? = 14$ $30 – 14 = 16$

$4 + 10 = 30 – 16$ $14 = 14$

ARGOPREP.COM

1. What number completes the number sentence?

$$34 - 20 = 10 + ?$$

_____

2.OA.1

2. What number completes the number sentence?

$$70 - 23 = 20 + ?$$

_____

2.OA.1

3. What number completes the number sentence?

$$35 + 25 = 100 - ?$$

_____

2.OA.1

4. What number completes the number sentence?

$$72 - 40 = 20 + ?$$

_____

2.OA.1

5. What number completes the number sentence?

$$15 + 40 = 35 + ?$$

_____

2.OA.1

6. What number completes the number sentence?

$$10 + 25 + 20 = 10 + ?$$

_____

2.OA.1

Be sure to check your work.

TIP of the DAY

1. What number completes the number sentence?

$$7 + 7 = 10 + ?$$

_____

1.OA.7
2.OA.1

2. What number completes the number sentence?

$$6 + 7 = 18 - ?$$

_____

1.OA.7
2.OA.1

3. What number completes the number sentence?

$$40 + 14 = 24 + ?$$

_____

1.OA.7
2.OA.1

4. What number completes the number sentence?

$$74 - 35 = 30 + ?$$

_____

1.OA.7
2.OA.1

5. What number completes the number sentence?

$$78 - 20 = 38 + ?$$

_____

1.OA.7
2.OA.1

6. What number completes the number sentence?

$$15 + 30 + 25 = 40 + ?$$

_____

1.OA.7
2.OA.1

DAY 6
CHALLENGE QUESTION

A. Find the sum of the numbers shown.

$$40 + 15 + 5 = ?$$

B. Find the same sum using the same two numbers.

_____ + _____ = ?

This week we are reviewing what we know from weeks 1-9. You can review weeks 1-9 to make sure you remember all of the skills.

You can find detailed video explanations to each problem in the book by visiting:
ArgoPrep.com

1. What set of numbers completes the sentence?

The number 295 has _____ hundreds _____ tens _____ ones

2.OA
2.NBT

2. What set of numbers completes the sentence?

The number 804 has _____ hundreds _____ tens _____ ones

2.OA
2.NBT

3. What number has 6 tens and 7 hundreds?

_____

2.OA
2.NBT

4. What symbol completes the number sentence?

Three hundred four _____ 3 hundreds 0 tens 2 ones

2.OA
2.NBT

5. What symbol completes the number sentence?

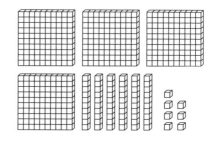

_____ Four hundred sixty one

2.OA
2.NBT

6. What sign completes the number sentence?

7 hundreds 1 ten nine ones _____ Seven hundred twenty eight

2.OA
2.NBT

TIP of the **DAY**

When doing different kinds of problems, take time to remember the same kinds of problems that you did before.

1. Jake had 7 crayons in a box. He put 9 more crayons in the box. How many crayons does Jake have now?

_____

2.OA.2

2. Sam had 16 stickers. She gave 9 stickers to her friend. How many stickers does Sam have now?

_____

2.OA.2

3. What is the sum of 9 and 6?

_____

2.OA.2

4. What is the difference of 12 and 3?

_____

2.OA.2

5. What number completes the number sentence?

$$7 + 6 = ?$$

_____

2.OA.2

6. What number completes the number sentence?

$$14 - 6 = ?$$

_____

2.OA.2

When doing different kinds of problems, take time to remember the same kinds of problems that you did before.

ARGOPREP.COM

1. What number does the array show?

_____

2.OA.4

2. What number sentence is shown using the model?

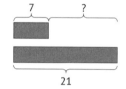

7   ?

21

_____

2.OA.1

Use the model for questions #3- #4.

3. What is the sum of the number in the model and 250?

_____

2.OA.7

4. What is the difference of the number in the model and 150?

_____

2.OA.7

5. What number is 10 less than 724?

_____

2.OA.8

6. What number is 100 more than 612?

_____

2.OA.8

When doing different kinds of problems, take time to remember the same kinds of problems that you did before.

ARGOPREP.COM

---

1. Kesha has 12 red bows, 13 blue bows and 15 green bows. What is the total number of bows that Kesha has?

_____

2.OA.6

---

2. There are 53 water bottles. The coach gave 24 water bottles to the children. How many water bottles are left?

_____

2.OA.5

---

3. Ali has 3 boxes of toy cars. Each box has 7 toy cars. Which number sentence could be used to find the total number of toy cars in the 3 boxes?

_____

2.OA.4

---

4. There are 15 cookies in the small box. There are 30 cookies in the big box. How many total cookies are in 2 small boxes and 2 big boxes?

_____

2.OA.6

---

5. There are 3 bags of grapes. Two bags have 24 grapes. The other bag has 35 grapes. What is the total number of grapes in the 3 bags?

_____

2.OA.6

---

6. The football team played 4 games. The table shows the number of points scored in each game.

Game	1	2	3	4
Points Scored	13	17	6	14

What is the total number of points scored in the 4 games?

_____

2.OA.6

When doing different kinds of problems, take time to remember the same kinds of problems that you did before.

Use the models for questions #1-4

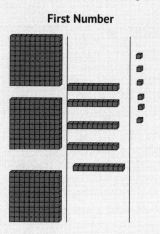
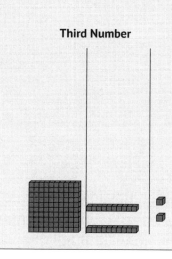

First Number   Second Number   Third Number

---

1. What is the sum of the First and Second Numbers?

_____

2.NBT.7

---

4. What is the sum of all three numbers?

_____

2.NBT.7

---

2. What is the difference of the Second and Third Numbers?

_____

2.NBT.7

---

5. What number completes the number sentence?

$$57 - 20 = 17 + ?$$

_____

2.OA.5

---

3. What is the number that is 100 more than the Second Number?

_____

2.NBT.7

---

6. What number completes the number sentence?

$$24 + 33 = 67 - ?$$

_____

2.OA.5

You can find detailed video explanations to each problem in the book by visiting:
ArgoPrep.com

MID ASSESSMENT

1. There were 6 apples in a bag. Then 5 more apples were put in the bag. How many total apples are now in the bag?

_____

2.OA.2

2. Ron had 11 baseball cards. He gave 9 to some friends. Which shows the number of baseball cards that Don has left?

_____

2.OA.2

3. What number completes the number sentence?

$$7 + 6 = 10 + ?$$

_____

2.OA.2

4. What number completes the number sentence?

$$6 + 6 = ?$$

_____

2.OA.2

5. Is the set of numbers all even? Why or why not?

$$2, 6, 10, 12$$

_____

2.OA.3

6. Is the sum of the number sentence odd? Why or why not?

$$4 + 6 = ?$$

_____

2.OA.3

7. What number completes the number sentence?

$$3 + 7 = 7 + ?$$

_____

2.OA.2

---

8. What number sentence could be used to find the answer to 9 + ? = 15?

_____

2.OA.2

---

9. In the morning there were 74 toy bears in a store. Then 37 toy bears were sold.

How many toy bears are now in the store?

_____

2.OA.1

---

10. The children brought in 28 leaves last week. Today they brought in 16 more. What is the total number of leaves?

_____

2.OA.1

---

11. What number sentence is shown using the model?

_____

2.OA.4

---

12. What number has 4 hundreds, 6 ones and 9 tens?

_____

2.NBT.1

13. What number has 7 tens and 8 ones?

_____

4.NBT.1

14. What is another way to show 100?

_____ tens

4.NBT.1a

15. What number is two hundred seventy?

_____

2.NBT.3

16. What number is 400 + 3?

_____

2.NBT.3

17. Which number has 6 ones 0 tens 3 hundreds?

_____

2.NBT.1

18. What symbol completes the number sentence?

Four hundred ninety six _____ 496

_____

2.NBT.4

ARGOPREP.COM

19. What symbol completes the number sentence?

913 _____ 9 hundreds 2 tens

_____

2.NBT.4

20. What set of five numbers starts at 65 and skip counts by 5?

_____ _____ _____ _____ _____

2.NBT.2

21. What set of five numbers starts at 325 and skip counts by 10?

_____ _____ _____ _____ _____

2.NBT.2

22. What number completes the number sentence?

46 + ? = 86

_____

2.OA.1

23. What is the sum of 37 + 7 + 12?

_____

2.OA.1

24. What number is 10 less than 621?

_____

2.NBT.8

25. What number is 100 more than 720?

_____

2.NBT.8

71

MID ASSESSMENT

Use the model for questions #26-27

First Number

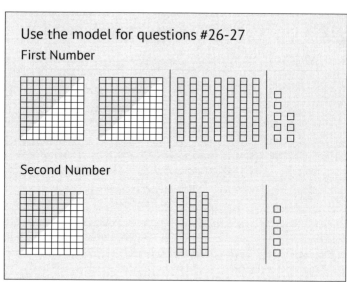

Second Number

Use the table for questions #28-30
The table shows the number of stickers in each box.

Color	Red	Blue	Green	Yellow
Number of Stickers in Each Box	18	22	24	16

26. What is the sum of the first number and the second number?

_____

2.NBT.7

27. What is the difference of the first number and the second number?

_____

2.NBT.7

28. What is the total number of stickers for 1 red and 2 blue boxes?

_____

2.NBT.6

29. What is the total number of stickers for 1 green and 2 yellow boxes?

_____

2.NBT.6

30. What is the total number of stickers for 1 of each color box?

2.NBT.6

This week we are measuring objects using a ruler. Lengths will be in inches and centimeters.

You can find detailed video explanations to each problem in the book by visiting:
ArgoPrep.com

1. What is the length of the paper clip?

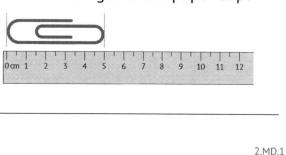

_____

2.MD.1

2. What is the length of the bow?

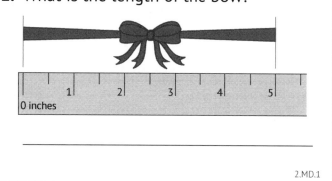

_____

2.MD.1

3. What is the length of the pencil?

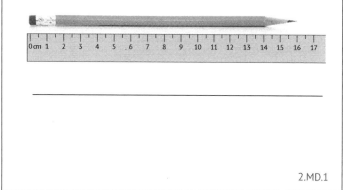

_____

2.MD.1

4. What is the length of the phone?

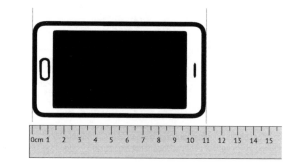

_____

2.MD.1

5. What is the length of the bat?

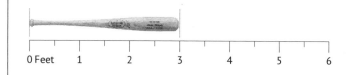

_____

2.MD.1

TIP of the DAY

When measuring, be sure to check if the unit is inches (in) centimeters (cm) feet (ft) or meters (m).

WEEK 11 · DAY 2

ARGOPREP.COM

1. Each paper clip is 1 inch in length.

What is the length of the marker?

_____

2.MD.2

2. Each pin is 1 centimeter in length.

What is the length of the crayon?

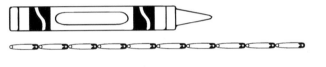

_____

2.MD.2

3. Each part of the fence is 1 meter in length.

What is the length of the fence?

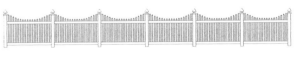

_____

2.MD.2

4. Each ruler has a length of 1 foot.

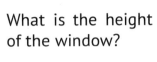

What is the height of the window?

_____

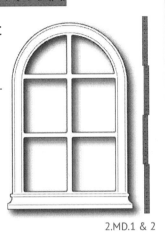

2.MD.1 & 2

5. Each pin has a length of 1 centimeter.

What is the length of the bow?

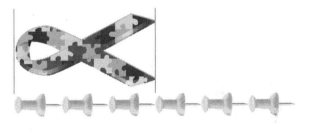

_____

2.MD.3

If we know the length of one thing, we can use it to measure other things.

TIP of the **DAY**

1. The lengths of a key and some beads are shown.

Complete the sentence.

The _____ is _____ cm. longer than the _____ .

2.MD.4

3. The lengths of paintbrush and feather are shown.

Complete the sentence.

The _____ is _____ in. longer than the _____ .

2.MD.4

2. The lengths of a ribbon and a pen are shown.

Complete the sentence.

The _____ is _____ in. longer than the _____ .

2.MD.4

4. The lengths of the nail and chain are shown.

Complete the sentence.

The _____ is _____ cm longer than the _____.

2.MD.4

When comparing two lengths, count up or back from one to the other to find the difference.

WEEK 11 · DAY 4

ARGOPREP.COM

1. What could show the length of a book?

12 _____

2.MD.3

4. Which could show the height of a child?

3 _____

2.MD.3

2. Which could show the length of a car?

15 _____

2.MD.3

5. Which could show the length of a banana?

9 _____

2.MD.3

3. Which could show how high, or the height of a room?

3 _____

2.MD.3

6. Which could show the length of a table?

2 _____

2.MD.3

We use inches and centimeters to measure smaller lengths. We use feet and meters to measure larger lengths.

WEEK 11 · DAY 5
ASSESSMENT

1. What is the length of the tag?

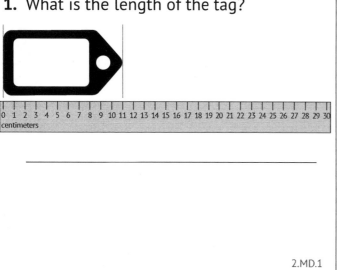

_____

2.MD.1

2. The clip has a length of 1 inch.

Which shows the length of the eraser?

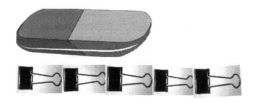

_____

2.MD.2

3. The lengths of the spoon and straw are shown.

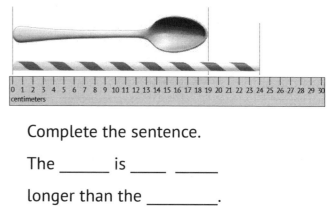

Complete the sentence.

The _____ is ____ _____

longer than the _____.

2.MD.4

4. What could show the height of a door?

8 _____

2.MD.3

5. What could show the length of candy bar?

6 _____

2.MD.3

DAY 6
CHALLENGE QUESTION

A crayon has a length of 4 inches. How many crayons could have the same length as a table with a length of 2 feet, or 24 inches?
How did you find your answer?

78

This week we are solving problems using measurement. Units will be inches, centimeters, feet and meters.

You can find detailed video explanations to each problem in the book by visiting:
ArgoPrep.com

WEEK 12 · DAY 1

ARGOPREP.COM

1. The length of a crayon is 4 inches. The length of a crayon box is 7 inches longer. What is the length of the crayon box?

_____

2.MD.5

2. The length of a small ribbon is 13 inches. The length of a big ribbon is 24 inches. What is the total length of the two ribbons?

_____

2.MD.5

3. The length of a toy truck is 19 centimeters. The length of a toy car is 7 centimeters shorter. What is the length of the toy car?

_____

2.MD.5

4. The length of a dog is 28 inches. The length of a cat is 14 inches. How much longer is the dog than the cat?

_____

2.MD.5

5. The length of the sidewalk in front of Kim's house is 43 feet long. The length of the side walk next door to Kim's house is 24 feet long. What is the total length of both sidewalks?

_____

2.MD.5

6. Jen is 37 inches tall. Her sister is 56 inches tall. How many inches taller is Jen's sister than Jen?

_____

2.MD.5

Use addition and subtraction to find the answers for questions about length.

80

1. The length of a book is 14 inches. This is 5 inches longer than the length of a bookmark. Write and solve a number sentence to show how to find the length of the bookmark.

_____

2.MD.5

2. The length of a red chain is 35 centimeters. The length of a green chain is 8 centimeters longer. Write and solve a number sentence to show how to find the total length of a red chain and a green chain.

_____

2.MD.5

3. There are two pictures on the wall. The length of one picture is 4 feet. The length of the other picture is 1 foot longer than the first picture. Write and solve a number sentence to show how to find the length of the longer picture.

_____

2.MD.5

Use the table for questions #4-6.
The table shows the length of some toy trains.

Train Color	Red	Blue	Green
Length in Inches	17	13	15

4. What is the total number of inches of 1 red and 1 blue train?

_____

2.MD.5

5. What is the total number of inches of 1 blue and 1 green train?

_____

2.MD.5

6. What is the total number of inches for 1 red, 1 blue and 1 green train?

_____

2.MD.5

When writing number sentences, read the question carefully to think about whether to add or subtract.

Use the table for questions #1-6

Tile Color	White	Black	Yellow	Orange
Length in Centimeters	13	17	12	15

Nick is putting some color tiles together. When he puts them together he wants to find the total length of the tiles.

1. What is the total length, in centimeters, of 2 white and 2 black tiles?

_____

2.MD.5

2. What is the total length, in centimeters, of 2 black and 2 orange tiles?

_____

2.MD.5

3. What is the total length, in centimeters, of 1 tiles of each color?

_____

2.MD.5

4. How many centimeters longer are 3 black tiles than 3 orange tiles?

_____

2.MD.5

5. How many centimeters longer are 2 orange tiles than 1 yellow tile?

_____

2.MD.5

6. What is the correct order of the color tiles, from shortest to longest in length?

Colors (Least to greatest length)

_____

2.MD.5

The length is how long something is. We can put lengths together to find the total length.

WEEK 12 · DAY 4

1. Kim has 3 pictures. Each picture has a length of 7 inches. What is the total length of the 3 pictures?

_____

2.MD.5

2. Maya's pencil case has a length of 16 centimeters. Her pencil has a length of 12 centimeters. How much longer is the pencil case than the pencil?

_____

2.MD.5

3. The wall in front of a house has a length of 26 feet. The wall in the back of the house has a length of 43 feet. What is the total length of both walls?

_____

2.MD.5

4. Vin wants to put 3 desks together. Each desk has a length of 24 inches. Which shows the total length of the 3 desks?

_____

2.MD.5

5. There are 2 trays on the table. The small tray has a length of 17 centimeters. The large tray has a length of 35 centimeters. What is the total length of the 2 trays?

_____

2.MD.5

6. There are 2 flags on the wall. Each flag has a length of 22 inches. The length between the flags is 8 inches.

Which shows the total length of the 2 flags and the length in between on the wall?

_____

2.MD.5

If the question asks what the length is and does not include the unit of measurement (inches, centimeters, feet, meters) then the answer should include the measurement.
What is the length in inches? 4
What is the length?   4 inches

83

Use the picture for questions #1-6
Ben's shoe has a length of 18 centimeters. His brother's shoe is 7 centimeters longer.

18 centimeters

1. Write and solve a number sentence to show how to find the length of Ben's brother's shoe.

_____

2.MD.5

2. Write and solve a number sentence to show how to find the total length of 1 of Ben's shoe and 1 of his brother's shoe.

_____

2.MD.5

3. What is the total length of 2 of Ben's shoes?

_____

2.MD.5

4. What is the total length of 2 of Ben's brother's shoes?

_____

2.MD.5

5. Ben has a pair of new shoes. Since he has grown, his new shoes are 4 centimeters longer. What the length of one of Ben's new shoes?

_____

2.MD.5

6. What is the length of 2 of Ben's new shoes?

_____

2.MD.5

DAY 6
CHALLENGE QUESTION

The square has 4 sides. The length of each side is 7 centimeters
What is the total length of the 4 sides of the square?

7 centimeters

WEEK 13

VIDEO EXPLANATIONS

ARGOPREP.COM

This week we are using number lines and number charts to find missing numbers. Numbers will be up to 100.

You can find detailed video explanations to each problem in the book by visiting:
ArgoPrep.com

1. A number line is shown.

5   6   8   9

What is the missing number?

_____

2.MD.6

2. A number line is shown.

16   17   18   ☐   20

What is the missing number?

_____

2.MD.6

3. A number chart is shown.

| 46 | 47 | ? | 49 | 50 |

What is the missing number?

_____

2.MD.6

4. A number chart is shown.

| 6 | ? | 8 | 9 | ? |

What two numbers complete the chart?

_____   _____

2.MD.6

5. A number chart is shown.

| 23 | 22 | 21 | 20 | ? |

What is the missing number?

_____

2.MD.6

TIP of the DAY

When finding missing numbers on a number line or a number chart, count the numbers that you see and look for a pattern.

WEEK 13 · DAY 2

ARGOPREP.COM

1. A number pattern is shown.

5	7	9	?

What is the missing number?

_____

2.MD.6

2. A number pattern is shown.

38	36	34	32	?

What is the fifth number?

_____

2.MD.6

3. A number pattern is shown.

15	20	25	30	?

What is the fifth number?

_____

2.MD.6

4. A number pattern is shown.

3   13   ⬭   33

What is the third number?

_____

2.MD.6

5. A number pattern is shown.

70   68   66   ?

What is the missing number?

_____

2.MD.6

When finding the missing number, find how much the number pattern is counting up or down by and how the pattern would keep going.

 # WEEK 13 · DAY 3

ARGOPREP.COM

1. A number chart is shown.

14	15
?	25

What is the missing number?

_____

2.MD.6

2. A number chart is shown.

?	63
72	?

What is the pair of missing numbers?

_____ _____

2.MD.6

3. A number chart is shown.

21	22	?
31	32	33
?	42	43

What is the pair of missing numbers?

_____ _____

2.MD.6

4. A number chart is shown.

78	77	76
68	?	66
58	57	?

What is the pair of missing numbers?

_____ _____

2.MD.6

5. A number chart is shown.

34	36	38	40
?	46	48	?
54	56	58	60

What is the pair of missing numbers?

_____ _____

2.MD.6

Sometimes we look down on number charts to find missing numbers. Think about the numbers around the missing number and look for patterns to help.

7	8	9
17	18	19
27	28	29

Counting by 1's across

Counting by 10's down

88

1. Rob was 38 inches tall. Then he grew. Now he is 49 inches tall. How many inches did Rob grow?

_____

2.MD.6

2. Lisa has a plant that is 14 centimeters high. Last month it was 9 centimeters high. How many centimeters did the plant grow?

_____

2.MD.6

3. A table is 3 feet high. On top of the table is a box that is 3 feet high. What is the height, the total number of feet, for the table and the box?

_____

2.MD.6

4. Jake is standing on a chair that is 24 inches high. Jake is 40 inches tall. While standing on the chair, he is now as tall as his sister.?

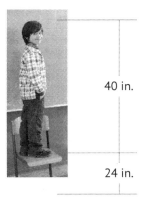

40 in.

24 in.

How many inches tall is Jake's sister?

_____

2.MD.6

5. There are 3 blocks as shown. Each block is 3 inches high. What is the height, the total number of inches, of the three blocks?

_____

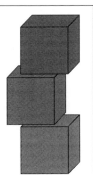

2.MD.6

When we measure how tall something is, it is like measuring length but up and down instead of across.

1. A number line is shown.

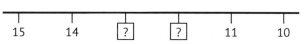

15   14   [?]   [?]   11   10

What is the missing pair of numbers?

_____ _____

2.MD.6

2. A number line is shown.

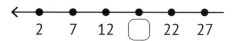

2   7   12   ◯   22   27

What is the missing number?

_____

2.MD.6

3. A number chart is shown.

28	30	?
38	40	42
48	?	52

What is the pair of missing numbers?

_____ _____

2.MD.6

4. The window has 2 parts. The length of each part is 22 inches.

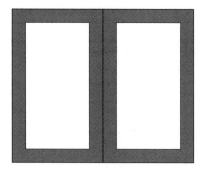

22 in.   22 in.

What is the total length, in inches, of the 2 windows?

_____

2.MD.6

5. Deb is 78 centimeters tall. She is 11 centimeters taller than her sister. What is the height, in centimeters, of her sister?

_____

2.MD.6

DAY 6
CHALLENGE QUESTION

A plant has a height of 23 centimeters. If the plant grows 4 centimeters each week, what would the height of the plant be 4 weeks from now?

This week we are telling and writing time using clocks. We will use time on an analog clock.

You can find detailed video explanations to each problem in the book by visiting:
ArgoPrep.com

1. What time is shown on the clock?

_____

2.MD.7

2. What time is shown on the clock?

_____

2.MD.7

3. What time is shown on the clock?

_____

2.MD.7

4. What time is shown on the clock?

_____

2.MD.7

5. What time is shown on the clock?

_____

2.MD.7

TIP **of the** DAY

When telling time, the big hand shows the hour and the small hand shows the minutes.

1. What time is shown on the clock?

_____

2.MD.7

2. What time is shown on the clock?

_____

2.MD.7

3. What time is shown on the clock?

_____

2.MD.7

4. What time is shown on the clock?

_____

2.MD.7

5. What time is shown on the clock?

_____

2.MD.7

On a clock you see the numbers 1-12.
Sometimes you can see tic marks in between
the numbers. Each tic mark is 1 minute.
As the minute hand moves, count by
5 minutes as it moves to the next number.
The time on this clock is 3:00. The minute
hand is on the 12. When the minute hand
moves from the 12 to 1, 5 minutes have passed.

3:00

3:05

1. What time is shown on the clock?

_____ minutes _____ _____

2.MD.7

2. What time is shown on the clock?

_____ minutes _____ _____

2.MD.7

3. What time is shown on the clock?

_____ minutes _____ _____

2.MD.7

4. What time is shown on the clock?

_____ minutes _____ _____

2.MD.7

5. What time is shown on the clock?

_____ minutes _____ _____

2.MD.7

TIP of the DAY

Another way to tell time is to tell the minutes after the hour that has just passed and the number of minutes to the next hour.
3:15 is also 15 minutes after 3
_3:15_
3:45 is 45 minutes after 3 or 15 minutes to 4.
_3:45_

94

1. Mark ate his breakfast at the time shown.

What time did Mark eat his breakfast? (including am or pm)

_____ _____

2.MD.7

2. After school, Jan did her homework at the time shown.

What time did Jan do her homework? (including am or pm)

_____ _____

2.MD.7

3. Name a time that children would most likely be sleeping?

_____

2.MD.7

4. Name a time that children would most likely be eating breakfast?

_____

2.MD.7

5. Name a time that children would most likely be in school?

_____

2.MD.7

6. Name a time that children would most likely be eating dinner?

_____

2.MD.7

The times are repeated 2 times each day. The a.m. times are for the first part of the day (from 12:00 midnight until 12:00 noon). The p.m. times are for the second part of the day (from 12:00 noon until 12:00 midnight).
Think about a.m. as early in the morning until lunch time and p.m. from lunch time until late night.

1. Kris ate dinner at the time shown.

What time did Kris eat dinner? (include am or pm)

_____ _____

2.MD.7

2. What time is shown on the clock?

_____

2.MD.7

3. What time is shown on the clock?

_____

2.MD.7

4. What time is shown on the clock?

_____

2.MD.7

5. What time is shown on the clock?

_____

2.MD.7

 # DAY 6
CHALLENGE QUESTION

Pete woke up at 7:30 am. Thirty minutes later he was ready for school. What time was Pete ready for school?

2.MD.7

WEEK 15

ARGOPREP.COM

VIDEO EXPLANATIONS

This week we are counting money. This includes dollars, quarters, dimes, nickels and pennies.

You can find detailed video explanations to each problem in the book by visiting:
ArgoPrep.com

WEEK 15 · DAY 1

ARGOPREP.COM

1. How much money is 6 pennies?

_____

2.MD.8

4. How much money is 2 quarters?

_____

2.MD.8

2. How much money is 5 nickels?

_____

2.MD.8

5. How much money is 4 nickels?

_____

2.MD.8

3. How much money is 3 dimes?

_____

2.MD.8

6. How much money is 3 dollar bills?

_____

2.MD.8

TIP of the DAY

When counting money, the coins we use are pennies, nickels, dimes and quarters. We can use bills like the one dollar bill. The coins and bills and the amounts are shown.

penny	nickel	dime	quarter	one dollar
1¢	5¢	10¢	25¢	$1.00
one cent	five cents	ten cents	twenty-five cents	one hundred cents

1. What amount of coins are equal to 12¢?

_____

2.MD.8

2. What amount of coins are equal to 35¢?

_____

2.MD.8

3. What amount of coins are equal to 60¢?

_____

2.MD.8

4. What amount of coins are equal to 85¢?

_____

2.MD.8

5. What amount of bills and coins are equal to $1.10?

_____

2.MD.8

6. What amount of bills and coins are equal to $1.50?

_____

2.MD.8

We can use different amount of coins to show the same amount.
5 pennies = 1 nickel 2 nickels = 1 dime 5 nickels = 1 quarter
2 dimes and 1 nickel = 1 quarter
4 quarters or 10 dimes or 20 nickels or 100 pennies = 1 dollar

1. What is the total amount of money?

_____

2.MD.8

2. What is the total amount of money?

_____

2.MD.8

3. What is the total amount of money?

_____

2.MD.8

4. What is the total amount of money?

_____

2.MD.8

5. What is the total amount of money?

_____

2.MD.8

TIP of the DAY

When finding the amount of money of dollars and coins, find all the amounts of each and add the amounts together.

1 dollar bill + 1 quarter + 3 nickels + 6 pennies
_$1.00 + 25¢ + 15¢ + 6¢= $1.46_

1. What shows 55¢ using the least number of coins?

_____

2.MD.8

2. What shows 63¢ using the least number of coins?

_____

2.MD.8

3. What shows 96¢ using the least number of coins?

_____

2.MD.8

4. What shows $1.31 using the least number of bills and coins?

_____

2.MD.8

5. What shows $2.22 using the least number of bills and coins?

_____

2.MD.8

When buying something, we sometimes try to use the largest coins possible so that we could use the least number of bills and coins.
For 30¢, you can use 3 dimes (3 coins) or 1 quarter and 1 nickel (2 coins)
For 85¢, you can use 8 dimes and 1 nickel (9 coins) or 3 quarters and 1 dime (4 coins)

TIP of the DAY

1. What is the total amount of 6 quarters?

_____

2.MD.8

2. What amount of coins are equal to 95¢?

_____

2.MD.8

3. What is the total amount of money?

_____

2.MD.8

4. What shows $1.38 using the least number of bills and coins?

_____

2.MD.8

5. What shows $3.73 using the least number of bills and coins?

_____

2.MD.8

DAY 6
CHALLENGE QUESTION

Mike has 68¢ in his pocket. He has exactly 7 coins. What are the coins that Mike has in his pocket?

WEEK 16

This week we are solving problems using line plots. We will use addition and subtraction to problem solve.

You can find detailed video explanations to each problem in the book by visiting:
ArgoPrep.com

ARGOPREP.COM

Use the Line Plot for questions #1-5

Number of Boxes with Different Amounts of Toys

```
                          X
              X           X
              X           X     X
    X    X    X    X      X     X
   _____
    0    1    2    3    4   5     6
```

Number of Toys in a Box

The children found some boxes. In some of the boxes there were different amounts of toys. The Xs show how many boxes had each number of toys.

2.MD.9

---

1. In how many boxes were there 6 toys?

_____

2.MD.9

---

2. In how many boxes were there 0 toys?

_____

2.MD.9

---

3. There were no boxes with what amount of toys?

_____

2.MD.9

---

4. What was the greatest amount of toys in a box?

_____

2.MD.9

---

5. The number of toys and the number of boxes were the same for what amount?

_____

2.MD.9

TIP of the DAY

Be sure to check the sign to determine if you will be adding, nding the sum, or subtracting, nding the difference.

ARGOPREP.COM

Use the line plot for questions #1-5.

Number of Students Taking Music Lessons

```
                    X
    X               X
    X       X       X
    X       X       X       X
    X       X       X       X
  ←─────────────────────────────
    2       3       4       5
              Grades
```

The line plot shows the number of students in grades 2-5 that are taking music lessons.

2.MD.9

1. How many students in grade 3 are taking lessons?

_____

2.MD.9

2. In what grade are there 4 students taking lessons?

_____

2.MD.9

3. In what grade are the most number of students taking lessons?

_____

2.MD.9

4. In what grade are the least number of students taking lessons?

_____

2.MD.9

5. How many students in grade 2 are taking lessons?

_____

2.MD.9

Make sure you check the titles of the line plot to understand what the amounts are and what is being counted.

Use the line plot for questions #1-5

Number of Pumpkins and What they Cost

```
                      X
         X            X
         X    X    X    X    X
        ─────────────────────────
        $1   $2   $3   $4   $5
```

Cost of the Pumpkins

There are pumpkins of different sizes for sale. The number of pumpkins that cost between $1 and $5 are shown on the line plot.

2.MD.9

1. How many pumpkins are being sold for $3?

_____

2.MD.9

2. How many pumpkins are being sold for $1?

_____

2.MD.9

3. How many pumpkins are being sold for $2?

_____

2.MD.9

4. There are 3 pumpkins being sold for the same cost. What is the cost?

_____

2.MD.9

5. What is the total number of pumpkins for sale?

_____

2.MD.9

If you count all of the X's you will know the total number of items in the line plot.

Use the line plot for questions #1-5
The lengths of some leaves were measured. The line plots show the number of leaves for each measurement.

Number of Leaves for Each Length

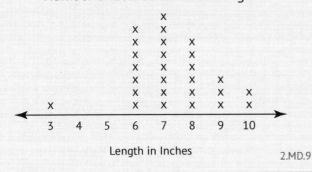

Length in Inches

2.MD.9

1. How many leaves measure 6 inches?

_____

2.MD.9

2. How many leaves measure 4 inches?

_____

2.MD.9

3. There are 3 leaves with the same measurement. What is the length?

_____

2.MD.9

4. One more leaf was measured and added to the line plot. The leaf measured 10 inches. What is the new number of leaves that measure 10 inches?

_____

2.MD.9

5. One more leaf was measured and added to the line plot. The leaf measured 5 inches. What is the new number of leaves that measure 5 inches?

_____

2.MD.9

When adding to the line plot, carefully look where the new X will be placed.

Sometimes there may be a symbol different that an X.
Use the line plot for questions #1-5

Number of Classes

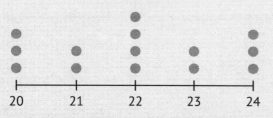

20   21   22   23   24

Number of Students in the Class

There are classes with student totals between 20 and 24. The line plot shows the classes that have each number of students.

2.MD.9

1. How many classes have 21 students?

_____

2.MD.9

2. There are 4 classes with the same number of students. What is the number of students in the classes?

_____

2.MD.9

3. What is the total number of classes?

_____

2.MD.9

4. One of the classes that had 23 students now has 1 more student. What is the new number of classes that now have 23 students?

_____

2.MD.9

5. How many classes have the greatest number of students?

_____

2.MD.9

DAY 6
CHALLENGE QUESTION

Some children are in the school band. There are 20 from Grade 3, 25 from Grade 4, and 28 from Grade 5. If a line plot was made, how many Xs would there be?

ARGOPREP.COM

Use the pictograph for questions #1-5

House	Number of Trees
Brown	🌲🌲🌲
Blue	🌲🌲🌲🌲🌲🌲
Green	🌲🌲
White	🌲🌲🌲

Key: 🌲 = 1 Tree

The children counted the number of trees in the back of 4 houses. The pictograph shows the number of trees for each house.

1. How many trees are in the back of the brown house?

_____

2.MD.10

2. What house has the greatest number of trees?

_____

2.MD.10

3. How many trees are in the back of the white house?

_____

2.MD.10

4. What house has the least number of trees?

_____

2.MD.10

5. How many total trees are in the back of the 4 houses?

_____

2.MD.10

When reading a pictograph, be sure to check the key to see what one picture is equal to.

110

Use the pictograph for questions #1-5

Box	Number of Pencils
Red	✏✏✏✏
Yellow	✏✏✏✏✏✏✏✏✏✏
Black	✏✏✏✏✏✏
Blue	✏✏✏✏✏✏✏✏

Key: ✏ = 1 Pencil

The students counted the number of pencils in 4 different color boxes. The pictograph shows the number of pencils in each box.

1. How many pencils are in the blue box?

_____

2.MD.10

2. What box has the least number of pencils?

_____

2.MD.10

3. How many total pencils are in the red and black boxes?

_____

2.MD.10

4. How many total pencils are in the yellow and blue boxes?

_____

2.MD.10

5. How many more pencils are in the yellow box than the red box?

_____

2.MD.10

Carefully read the pictograph when adding and subtracting the numbers that show the amounts.

Use the bar graph for questions #1-5

Favorite Sport

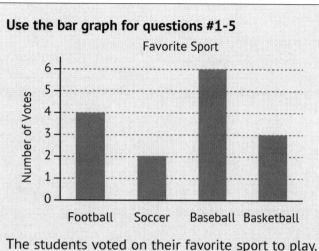

The students voted on their favorite sport to play. The bar graph shows the number of students that voted for each sport.

2.MD.10

1. How many votes were for Basketball?

_____

2.MD.10

2. What sport had 2 votes?

_____

2.MD.10

3. How many votes were for Football?

_____

2.MD.10

4. What sport had the greatest number of votes?

_____

2.MD.10

5. What sport has the least number of votes?

_____

2.MD.10

TIP of the DAY

When reading a bar graph, be sure to look across from the number to see the bar height and then look down to see what is being measured.

112

ARGOPREP.COM

Use the Bar Graph for questions #1-5
The students made a bar graph to show their birthdays in each season.

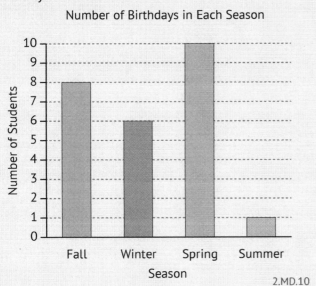

Number of Birthdays in Each Season

2.MD.10

3. What is the total number of students with birthdays in Fall and Summer?

_____

2.MD.10

1. How many students have winter birthdays?

_____

2.MD.10

2. What season has 8 students with birthdays?

_____

2.MD.10

4. What is the total number of students with birthdays in Winter and Spring?

_____

2.MD.10

5. How many more students have birthdays in Fall than in Winter?

_____

2.MD.10

When using the bar graph to add and subtract the bar heights, write the heights down and then add or subtract.

Use the bar graph for questions #1-5
The bar graph shows the number of students and their folder color

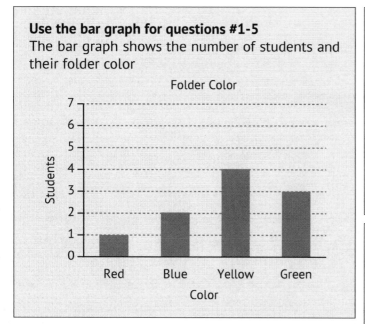

Folder Color

1. How many students have blue folders?

_____

2.MD.10

2. The greatest number of students have what color folder?

_____

2.MD.10

3. How many more students have green folders than red folders?

_____

2.MD.10

4. The least number of students have what color folder?

_____

2.MD.10

5. What is the total number of folders?

_____

2.MD.10

DAY 6
CHALLENGE
QUESTION

A total of 24 folders were given to students in 4 colors. There were the same number of folders for each color. How many folders were there in each of the 4 colors?

114

This week we are counting the number of sides and angles in shapes. We will use shapes from 3 sides to 6 sides.

You can find detailed video explanations to each problem in the book by visiting:
ArgoPrep.com

1. A shape is shown.

How many sides does the shape have?

_____

2.G.1

3. A shape is shown.

How many sides does the shape have?

_____

2.G.1

2. A shape is shown.

How many sides does the shape have?

_____

2.G.1

4. A shape is shown.

How many sides does the shape have?

_____

2.G.1

Flat shapes have straight sides that we can count.

1. A shape is shown.

How many sides and how many angles does the shape have?

_____ sides _____ angles

2.G.1

2. A shape is shown.

How many sides and how many angles does the shape have?

_____ sides _____ angles

2.G.1

3. A shape is shown.

How many sides and angles does the shape have?

_____ sides _____ angles   2.G.1

4. A shape is shown

How many sides and angles does the shape have?

_____ sides _____ angles

2.G.1

5. How many angles does a 6 sided shape have?

_____

2.G.1

Shapes that are made of straight sides have angles where the sides bend. The number of angles are the same as the number of sides.

TIP of the DAY

117

1. Tell if the statement is True or False and why.

This shape does NOT have 4 sides.

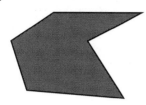

_____

2.G.1

3. Tell if the statement is True or False and why.

This shape does NOT have 6 sides.

_____

2.G.1

2. Tell if the statement is True or False and why.

This shape does have 6 sides.

_____

2.G.1

4. Tell if the statement is True or False and why.

The shape does NOT have 6 sides.

_____

2.G.1

Be careful with questions that ask NOT.

1. Two shapes are shown.

How many total sides do both shapes have?

_____

2.G.1

2. Two shapes are shown.

How many total sides do both shapes have?

_____

2.G.1

3. Two shapes are shown.

Shape 1   Shape 2

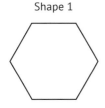

How many more sides does Shape 1 have than Shape 2?

_____

2.G.1

4. Three shapes are shown.

Shape 1   Shape 2   Shape 3

Which shows the correct order of the Shapes from least number of sides to greatest number of sides?

_____ _____ _____

2.G.1

5. Three shapes are shown.

Shape 1   Shape 2   Shape 3

Which two shapes have the same number of sides?

_____

2.G.1

Read the questions carefully if you need to add or subtract. Write down the numbers then add or subtract.

119

WEEK 18 · DAY 5
ASSESSMENT

1. A shape is shown.

How many sides does the shape have?

_____

2.G.1

3. Two shapes are shown.

Shape 1   Shape 2

What is the total number of sides for Shape 1 and Shape 2?

_____

2.G.1

2. Is this a shape with all straight sides? Why or why not?

_____

2.G.1

4. Three shapes are shown.

What is the total number of sides for all three shapes?

_____

2.G.1

DAY 6
CHALLENGE
QUESTION

How many total sides are there for a 3, 4, 5 and 6 sided shape?

_____

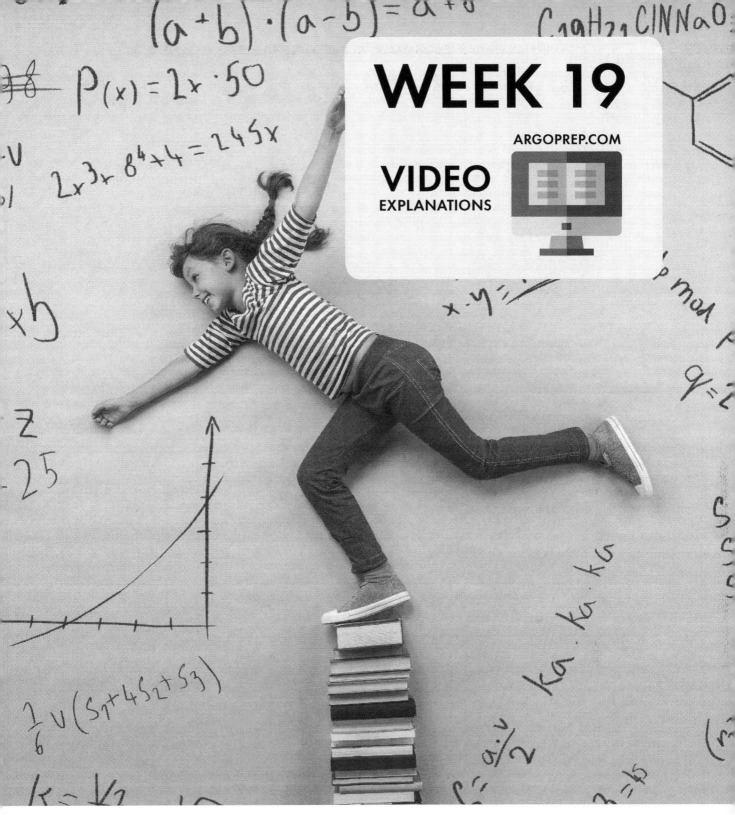

WEEK 19

ARGOPREP.COM

VIDEO
EXPLANATIONS

This week we are counting squares and finding equal parts of a shape. We will use addition to find the total number of squares.

You can find detailed video explanations to each problem in the book by visiting:
ArgoPrep.com

1. What is the total number of squares?

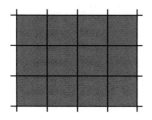

_____

2.G.2

2. What is the total number of squares?

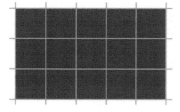

_____

2.G.2

3. What is the total number of squares?

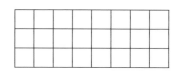

_____

2.G.2

4. What is the total number of squares?

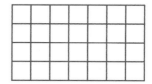

_____

2.G.2

Rectangles can be made up of equal sized squares. The squares going across are called rows. The squares going up and down are called columns.

 TIP of the DAY

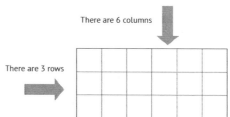

There are 6 columns

There are 3 rows

3 rows of 6 columns
6 + 6 + 6 = 18 total squares

122

1. What number sentence can be used to find the total number of squares?

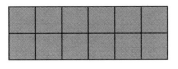

_____

2.G.2

2. What number sentence can be used to find the total number of squares?

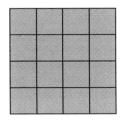

_____

2.G.2

3. What number sentence can be used to find the total number of squares?

_____

2.G.2

4. How many rows are there and how many squares are in each row?

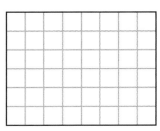

There are _____ rows
of _____ squares

2.G.2

5. What is the total number of squares?

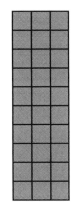

_____

2.G.2

To find the total number of squares, you can add the row totals or add the column total.

TIP of the DAY

123

1. Does the shape have equal parts?

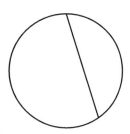

_____

2.G.3

3. What is the shape cut into?

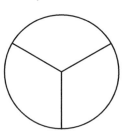

_____

2.G.3

2. Is the shape cut into halves?

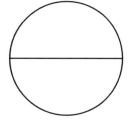

_____

2.G.3

4. What is the shape cut into?

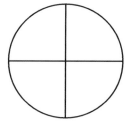

_____

2.G.3

TIP of the **DAY**

Shapes can have equal parts. We count the number of equal parts that the shape has. Two equal parts are called halves. Three equal parts are called thirds. Four equal parts are called fourths.

1. A shape is shown.

Describe the shape.

2.G.3

_____

2. A shape is shown.

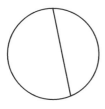

Describe the shape

2.G.3

_____

3. A shape is shown.

Describe the shape.   2.G.3

_____

4. A shape is shown.

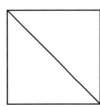

Describe the shape.

_____

2.G.3

5. A shape is shown.

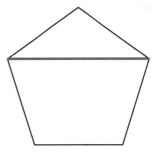

Describe the shape.

_____

2.G.3

Count the number of equal parts for shapes to describe the parts of the shape.

1. What is the total number of squares?

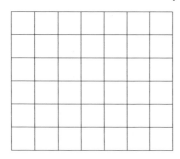

_____

2.G.2

2. What is the total number of squares?

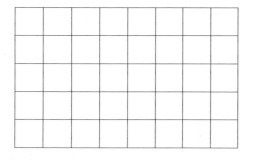

_____

2.G.2

3. A shape is shown.

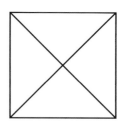

Describe the shape.

_____

2.G.3

4. A shape is shown.

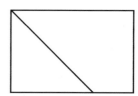

Describe the shape.

_____

2.G.3

 # DAY 6
CHALLENGE QUESTION

A shape is cut into 3 equal parts. What do we call each part?

This week we are reviewing what we know from weeks 11-19. You can review weeks 11-19 to make sure you remember all of the skills.

You can find detailed video explanations to each problem in the book by visiting:
ArgoPrep.com

1. What is the length of the crayon?

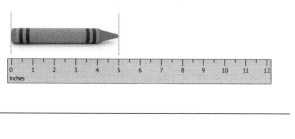

_____

2.MD.1

2. What is the length of the fish?

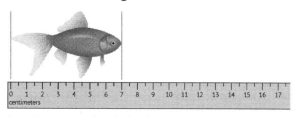

_____

2.MD.1

3. The eraser cap has a length of 1 inch.

What is the length of the bookmark?

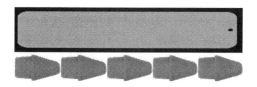

_____

2.MD.2

4. The lengths of a glue stick and a toothbrush are shown.

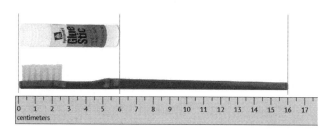

How much longer is the toothbrush than the glue stick?

_____

2.MD.4

5. What could the length of a room be?

8 _____

2.MD.3

TIP of the **DAY**

When doing different kinds of problems, take time to remember the same kinds of problems that you did before.

1. The length of a window is 2 feet. The length of the wall next to the window is 12 feet. What is the total length of the window and the wall?

_____

2.MD.5

2. The height of desk is 26 inches. A boy is 16 inches taller than the desk. What is the height of the boy?

_____

2.MD.5

3. A number line is shown.

94 ____ 96 97 98 99 ____ 101

What is the missing pair of numbers?

_____

2.MD.6

4. A number chart is shown.

37	38	39	40
?	48	49	50
57	58	59	?

What two numbers complete the chart?

_____

2.MD.6

5. A number chart is shown.

28	30	?	34	?	38

What pair of numbers complete the chart?

_____

2.MD.6

When doing different kinds of problems, take time to remember the same kinds of problems that you did before.

1. What is the time on the clock?

2.MD.7

2. What is the time on the clock?

2.MD.7

3. What amount of money is equal to 3 dollars 5 dimes, 1 nickels and 3 pennies?

2.MD.8

4. What is the amount of money equal to 98 using the least number of coins?

2.MD.8

5. What is the total amount of money?

2.MD.8

When doing different kinds of problems, take time to remember the same kinds of problems that you did before.

ARGOPREP.COM

3. What grade had the most pictures?

_____

2.MD.10

Use the bar graph for #1-5
The bar graph shows the number of pictures painted by students in grades 1-4 in art class.

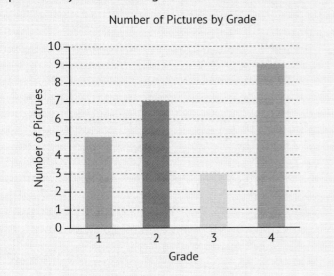

Number of Pictures by Grade

1. What is the number of pictures from Grade 1 students?

_____

2.MD.10

2. What grade has 7 pictures?

_____

2.MD.10

4. How many more pictures were from Grade 1 than from Grade 3?

_____

2.MD.10

5. What is the total amount of pictures?

_____

2.MD.10

When doing different kinds of problems, take time to remember the same kinds of problems that you did before.

1. What is the total number of squares?

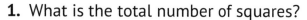

_____

2.G.2

2. A shape is shown.

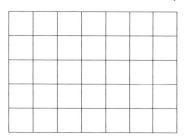

How many sides does the shape have?

_____

2.G.1

3. A shape is shown.

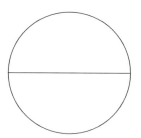

Is the shape cut into equal parts?

_____

2.G.3

4. A shape shown.

Is the shape cut into equal parts?

_____

2.G.3

DAY 6
CHALLENGE QUESTION

Cut the shape into fourths.

THE END!

Assessment

ARGOPREP.COM

VIDEO
EXPLANATIONS

Great job finishing all 20 weeks! You should be ready for any test. Try this assessment to see how much you've learned - good luck!

1. There were 7 baseballs in a box. Then 9 more baseballs were put in the box. What is the total number of baseballs in the box?

_____

2.OA.2

2. Jay saved 17 dollars. He spent 8 dollars. How many dollars does Jay have left?

_____

2.OA.2

3. What number completes the number sentence?

$$7 + 6 = 10 + ?$$

_____

2.OA.2

4. What is the sum of 7 + 7? Is the sum even or odd?

_____ _____

2.OA.3

5. Last month there were 65 toy tigers in a store. Then 36 were sold.

How many toy tigers are now in the store?

_____

2.NBT.5

6. The teacher had 25 books last week. Today the teacher brought in 16 more. How many books are there now?

_____

2.NBT.5

7. What number sentence is shown using the model?

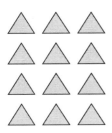

_____

2.OA.4

8. What number has 8 tens, 3 ones and 1 hundred?

_____

2.NBT.1

9. What shows the number three hundred nine?

_____

2.NBT.3

10. What symbol completes the number sentence?

Four hundred seventy six? 467

_____

2.NBT.4

11. What set of four numbers starts at 225 and skip counts by 10?

_____

2.NBT.8

12. What number completes the number sentence?

16 + ? = 56

_____

2.NBT.5

13. What is the sum of 58 + 5 + 18?

_____

2.NBT.6

14. What number is 10 more than 345?

_____

2.NBT.8

Use the model for questions #15-16.

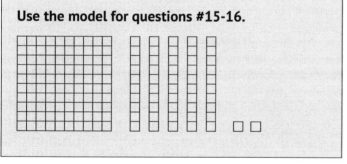

15. What is the sum of the number in the model and 243?

_____

2.NBT.7

16. Which shows the difference of the number in the model and 71?

_____

2.NBT.7

Use the figure for #17-19.
The lengths of a crayon and pencil are shown.

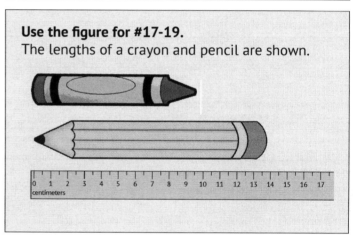

17. What is the length of the pencil?

_____ centimeters

2.MD.4

138

18. How much longer is the length of the pencil than the length of the crayon?

_____ centimeters

2.MD.4

19. What is the sum of the two lengths?

_____ centimeters

2.MD.5

20. What could be the length of a soccer field?

110 _____

2.MD.3

21. The length of a toy animal is 14 inches. The length of toy truck is 5 inches longer.

Which shows the length of the toy truck?

_____ inches

2.MD.5

22. A number chart is shown.

31	32	33
?	42	43
51	?	53

What pair of numbers completes the chart?

_____

2.MD.6

23. What is the time on the clock?

_____

2.MD.7

139

24. What is the total amount of money?

_____

2.MD.8

25. Show $1.29 using the least number of coins.

_____

2.MD.8

Use the pictograph for questions #26-27.
The students that had dogs were asked to tell if their dog was small, medium, or large sized. The pictograph shows the number of dogs for each size.

Dog Sizes	
Small Dogs	🐾 🐾 🐾
Medium Dogs	🐾 🐾
Large Dogs	🐾 🐾 🐾

Key: 🐾 = 1 Dog

26. How many more small dogs than medium dogs?

_____

2.MD.10

27. What is the total number of dogs?

_____

2.MD.10

28. What is the total number of squares?

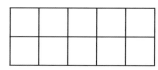

_____

2.G.2

29. The shape has how many sides?

_____

2.G.1

30. What is the shape cut into?

_____

2.G.3

ANSWER KEYS

VIDEO
EXPLANATIONS

ARGOPREP.COM

ANSWER KEYS

For more practice with 2nd Grade Math, be sure to check out our other book, Argo Brothers Math Workbook Grade 2: Multiple Choice

WEEK 1

DAY 1
1. 469
2. 5
3. tens
4. 269
5. 20
6. hundreds, ones

DAY 2
1. 10
2. 560
3. 18
4. 5 hundreds, 0 tens, 0 ones
5. tens
6. one ten or ten ones

DAY 3
1. four hundred twenty-three
2. 400 + 70
3. 627
4. eight hundred thirty-two
5. 100 + 70 + 4

DAY 4
1. 500, 600, 700, 800, 900
2. 50, 55, 60, 65, 70
3. by ten (10)
4. 550, 555, 560, 565, 570
5. 300, 400, 500, 600, 700
6. 80, 100, 110

DAY 5
1. 10 tens = 1 hundred or 100 = 100
2. one hundred seventy
3. 67
4. 200 + 40 + 1
5. skip counted by 10, 400 is missing
6. 8 hundreds, 9 tens, 0 ones

DAY 6
380, three hundred eighty, 300 + 80

WEEK 2

DAY 1
1. <
2. <
3. >
4. =
5. >

DAY 2
1. <
2. <
3. =
4. <
5. >

DAY 3
1. 4,5,6,7,8 or 9
2. 6,7,8 or 9
3. 0,1,2,3,4,5 or 6
4. Blue
5. any number 162-178

DAY 4
1. =
2. >
3. 8 (586)
4. =
5. <
6. <

DAY 5
1. =
2. >
3. 0,1,2,3,4,5 or 6
4. any number 410 – 414
5. >
6. <

DAY 6
532, 532 > 422

WEEK 3

DAY 1
1. 9
2. 13
3. 5 + 4 = 9
4. 3 + 4 = 7
5. 7
6. 4 + 7

DAY 2
1. 11
2. 6 + 9 = 15
3. 5+5, 6+4, 7+3, 8+2, 9+1, 10+0
4. 6 + 2 = 8 or 8 – 6 = 2
5. 12
6. 12

DAY 3
1. 4 + 4 = 8
2. 6 + 7 = 13
3. 7 + 7 = 14 or 2+2+2+2+2+2+2 = 14.
4. 7 + 6 = 13
5. 8 + 8 = 16
6. 10 + 10 = 20

DAY 4
1. 12
2. 10 + 1 = 11
3. 9 + 7 = 16, 10 +6 = 16
4. 7+8 or 9+6 or 10+5 or 11+4 or 12+3 or 13+2 or 14+1 or 15+0
5. 14
6. 12

DAY 5
1. 16
2. 16
3. 5+5 = 10, 6+4 = 10, 7+3 = 10 8+2 =10, 9+1 = 10. 10+0 = 10
4. 2+2 or 3+3 or 4+4 or 5+5 or 6+6 or 7+7 or 8+8 or 9+9
5. 8+3 and 3+8 or any pair of numbers that are used in two different orders
6. 9+7 = 16, 10+6 = 16

DAY 6
7+7 6+8 9+5

WEEK 4

DAY 1
1. 5
2. 6
3. 15 – 7 = 8
4. 7
5. 7
6. 18 – 9 = 9

DAY 2
1. 9
2. 8
3. 6
4. 7 – 3 = 4
5. 8
6. 7

DAY 3
1. 6 – 5 = 1
2. 14
3. 11 – 4 = 7
4. 9 is 6 more than 3
5. 17
6. 16

DAY 4
1. 5+5+5= 15 or 3+3+3+3+3 = 15
2. 7+7+7 = 21 or 3+3+3+3+3+3+3= 21
3. 2+2+2+2+2+2 = 12 or 6+6 =12
4. 3+3+3+3 = 12
5. 4+4+4+4 = 16

DAY 5
1. 6 – 3 = 3
2. 8 – 2 = 6 or 6 + 2 = 8
3. 6+6+6+6 = 24 or 4+4+4+4+4+4 = 24
4. 9 + 4 = 13 or 13 – 9 = 4
5. 7 and 0, 8 and 1, 9 and 2, 10 and 3, 11 and 4, 12 and 5, 13 and 6, 14 and 7, 15 and 8, 16 and 9

DAY 6
8 + 7 = 15 8 – 7 = 1

WEEK 5

DAY 1
1. 0, 2, 4
2. 1, 3
3. 0, 2, 4, 6, 8
4. 1, 3, 5, 7, 9
5. 11 and 12, 13 and 14, 13 and 12

DAY 2
1. 12, 14
2. 11, 13
3. 17, 19
4. 16, 18
5. 9, 11
6. 10, 12

DAY 3
1. 1+1 = 2, 2+2 = 4, 3+1 = 4, 2+0 = 2
2. 0+1 = 1, 1+2 =3, 0+3 = 3
3. 4+2 = 6, 3+3 = 6, 5+1 = 6, 4+4 = 8, 5+3 = 8, 6+2 = 8, 7+1 = 8, 8+0 = 8
4. 5+7 = 12, 7+7 = 14
5. 6+6 = 12, 6+8 = 14

DAY 4
1. 8
2. 13
3. 13 – 4 = 9
4. 7 + 4 = 11
5. 8

DAY 5
1. odd + odd = even
2. odd + odd = even
3. even + even = even
4. even 10, 12 odd 11
5. 6
6. 7 + 8 = 15

DAY 6
odd 5 + 6 = 11 , 7 + 8 = 15, the sum will not make a pair, there is always one more than a pair

WEEK 6

DAY 1
1. 73
2. 14
3. 38
4. 75
5. 32
6. 52

DAY 2
1. 66
2. 79
3. 31
4. 45
5. 67
6. 63

DAY 3
1. 72
2. 52
3. 82
4. 52
5. 53
6. 73

DAY 4
1. 38
2. 18
3. 48
4. 22
5. 37
6. 49

DAY 5
1. 54
2. 11
3. 65
4. 77
5. 26
6. 63

DAY 6
Two numbers with a sum of 65 for example, 30 + 35, 40 + 25
The correct difference of the two numbers

WEEK 7

DAY 1
1. 82
2. 53
3. 86
4. 52
5. 56
6. 75

DAY 2
1. 62
2. 66
3. 65
4. 58
5. Blue
6. White

DAY 3
1. 80
2. 100
3. 68
4. 67
5. 90

DAY 4
1. 448
2. 161
3. 477
4. 515
5. 281
6. 719

DAY 5
1. 86
2. 84
3. 50
4. 730
5. 773
6. 195

DAY 6
293

WEEK 8

DAY 1	DAY 2	DAY 3	DAY 4	DAY 5
1. 373	**1.** 435	**1.** 170	**1.** 435	**1.** 918
2. 438	**2.** 222	**2.** 78	**2.** 75	**2.** 514
3. 818	**3.** 445	**3.** 390	**3.** 754	**3.** 563
4. 328	**4.** 815	**4..** 62	**4.** 72	**4.** 309
5. 244	**5.** 691	**5.** 118	**5.** 424	**5.** 898
6. 508			**6.** 128	**6.** 208

DAY 6

A. 579
B. 333

WEEK 9

DAY 1	DAY 2	DAY 3	DAY 4	DAY 5
1. 2	**1.** 5	**1.** 23	**1.** 4	**1.** 4
2. 8	**2.** 8	**2.** 13	**2.** 27	**2.** 5
3. 5	**3.** 2	**3.** 33	**3.** 40	**3.** 30
4. 5	**4.** 7	**4.** 3	**4.** 12	**4.** 9
5. 2	**5.** 18	**5.** 30	**5.** 20	**5.** 20
6. 8	**6.** 21	**6.** 35	**6.** 45	**6.** 30

DAY 6

A. 60 B. 30 + 30 or 40 + 20
or any pair that equals 60

WEEK 10

DAY 1	DAY 2	DAY 3	DAY 4	DAY 5
1. 2 hundreds, 9 tens, 5 ones	**1.** 16	**1.** 30	**1.** 40	**1.** 598
2. 8 hundreds, 0 tens, 4 ones	**2.** 7	**2.** 7 + 14 = 21 or 21 – 7 = 14	**2.** 29	**2.** 120
3. 760	**3.** 15	**3.** 526	**3.** 21	**3.** 342
4. >	**4.** 9	**4.** 126	**4.** 90	**4.** 720
5. >	**5.** 13	**5.** 714	**5.** 83	**5.** 20
6. <	**6.** 8	**6.** 712	**6.** 50	**6.** 10

Mid Assessment

1. 11	**7.** 3	**13.** 78	**20.** 65, 70, 75, 80, 85	**27.** 143
2. 2	**8.** 15 – 9 = 6	**14.** ten tens	**21.** 325, 335, 345, 355, 365	**28.** 62
3. 3	**9.** 37	**15.** 270	**22.** 40	**29.** 56
4. 12	**10.** 44	**16.** 403	**23.** 56	**30.** 80
5. yes, even numbers end in 0, 2, 4, 6, 8	**11.** 4 + 4 + 4 = 12 or 3 + 3 + 3 + 3 = 12	**17.** 306	**24.** 611	
6. no, even numbers end in 0, 2, 4, 6, 8	**12.** 496	**18.** =	**25.** 820	
		19. <	**26.** 413	

WEEK 11

DAY 1
1. 5 cm
2. 5 in
3. 16 cm
4. 11 cm
5. 3 ft

DAY 2
1. 4 in
2. 7 cm
3. 6 m
4. 4 ft
5. 3 cm

DAY 3
1. key, 2, beads
2. ribbon, 3, pen
3. paintbrush, 5, feather
4. chain, 10, nail

DAY 4
1. in
2. ft
3. m
4. ft
5. in
6. m or ft

DAY 5
1. 11 cm
2. 3 in
3. straw, 5, spoon
4. ft
5. in

DAY 6
6 crayons

WEEK 12

DAY 1
1. 11 in
2. 37 in
3. 12 cm
4. 14 in
5. 67 ft
6. 19 in

DAY 2
1. 14 − 5 = 9 in
2. 35 + 35 + 8 = 78 cm or 35 + 43 = 78 cm
3. 4 + 1 = 5 ft
4. 30 cm
5. 28
6. 45

DAY 3
1. 60
2. 64
3. 57
4. 6
5. 18
6. Yellow, White, Orange, Black

DAY 4
1. 21 in
2. 4 cm
3. 69 ft
4. 72 in
5. 52 cm
6. 52 in

DAY 5
1. 18 + 7 = 25 cm
2. 18 + 18 + 7 = 43 cm or 18 + 25 = 43 cm
3. 36 cm
4. 50 cm
5. 22 cm
6. 44 cm

DAY 6
28 cm

WEEK 13

DAY 1
1. 7
2. 19
3. 48
4. 7, 10
5. 19

DAY 2
1. 11
2. 30
3. 35
4. 23
5. 64

DAY 3
1. 24
2. 62, 73
3. 23, 41
4. 67, 56
5. 44, 50

DAY 4
1. 11 in
2. 5 cm
3. 6 ft
4. 64 in
5. 9 in

DAY 5
1. 13, 12
2. 17
3. 32, 50
4. 44 in
5. 67 cm

DAY 6
39 cm

WEEK 14

DAY 1
1. 8:00
2. 2:30
3. 7:15
4. 9:05
5. 2:15

DAY 2
1. 7:10
2. 8:05
3. 4:10
4. 12:45
5. 10:50

DAY 3
1. 10 after 6
2. 5 after 11
3. 20 before 7
4. 5 before 5
5. 15 before 8

DAY 4
1. 7:30 am
2. 3:30 pm
3. any time between 9:00 pm and 9:00 am
4. any time between 7:00 am and 10:00 am
5. any time between 8:00 am and 3:00 pm
6. any time between 4:00 pm and 7:00 pm

DAY 5
1. 5:00 pm
2. 9:30
3. 12:20
4. 11:45
5. 1:30

DAY 6
8:00 am

WEEK 15

DAY 1
1. 6 cents
2. 25 cents
3. 30 cents
4. 50 cents
5. 20 cents
6. 3 dollars

DAY 2
1. 12 pennies or 1 dime and 2 pennies or 2 nickels and 2 pennies
2. 1 quarter 1 dime or 3 dimes 1 nickel
3. 6 dimes or 2 quarters 1 dime or 2 quarters 2 nickels
4. 3 quarters 1 dime or 8 dimes 1 nickel
5. 1 dollar 1 dime or 4 quarters 1 dime
6. 1 dollar 2 quarters or 6 quarters or 1 dollar 5 dimes

DAY 3
1. $2.94
2. $2.03
3. $2.71
4. $4.05
5. $3.52

DAY 4
1. 2 quarters 1 nickel
2. 2 quarters 1 dime 3 nickels
3. 3 quarters 2 dimes 1 penny
4. 1 dollar 1 quarter 1 nickel 1 penny
5. 2 dollars 2 dimes 2 pennies

DAY 5
1. $1.50
2. 3 quarters 2 dimes or 9 dimes 1 nickel
3. $4.76
4. 1 dollar 1 quarter 1 dime 3 pennies
5. 3 dollars 2 quarters 2 dimes 3 pennies

DAY 6
2 quarters 1 dime 1 nickel 3 pennies

WEEK 16

DAY 1
1. 2
2. 1
3. 4
4. 6
5. 3

DAY 2
1. 3
2. 2
3. 4
4. 5
5. 4

DAY 3
1. 1
2. 2
3. 1
4. $4
5. 8

DAY 4
1. 7
2. 0
3. 9 in
4. 3
5. 1

DAY 5
1. 2
2. 22
3. 14
4. 3
5. 3

DAY 6
73

WEEK 17

DAY 1
1. 3
2. Blue
3. 4
4. Green
5. 15

DAY 2
1. 8
2 Red
3. 10
4. 18
5. 6

DAY 3
1. 3
2. Soccer
3. 4
4. Baseball
5. Soccer

DAY 4
1. 6
2. Fall
3. 9
4. 16
5. 2

DAY 5
1. 2
2. Yellow
3. 2
4. Red
5. 10

DAY 6
6 folders

WEEK 18

DAY 1
1. 3
2. 4
3. 6
4. 5

DAY 2
1. 4, 4
2. 0, 0
3. 3, 3
4. 4, 4
5. 6

DAY 3
1 True, has 6 sides
2. True, has 6 sides
3. True, has 5
4. False, has 6

DAY 4
1. $3 + 5 = 8$
2. $4 + 4 = 8$
3. 2
4. Shape 3, 1, 2
5. Shape 2 and 3

DAY 5
1. 4,
2. no, has a curved or round side
3. $4 + 3 = 7$
4. $6 + 6 + 4 = 16$

DAY 6
18 sides

WEEK 19

DAY 1
1. 12
2. 15
3. 24
4. 28

DAY 2
1. 6 + 6 or 2 + 2 + 2 + 2 + 2 + 2 = 12
2. 4+4+4+4 = 16
3. 10+10+10+10+10+10= 60 or 6+6+6+6+6+6+6+6+6+6 = 60
4. 6 rows of 8 squares
5. 30

DAY 3
1. no
2. yes
3. thirds
4. fourths

DAY 4
1. cut into thirds or three equal parts
2. unequal parts
3. cut into fourths or four equal parts
4. cut into halves or two equal parts
5. unequal parts

DAY 5
1. 42
2. 40
3. cut into fourths or four equal parts
4. unequal parts

DAY 6
thirds

WEEK 20

DAY 1
1. 5 in
2. 7 cm
3. 5 in
4. 10 cm
5. ft or m

DAY 2
1. 14 ft
2. 42 in
3. 95, 100
4. 47, 60
5. 32, 36

DAY 3
1. 4:30
2. 5:45
3. $3.58
4. 3 quarters 2 dimes 3 pennies
5. $4.16

DAY 4
1. 5
2. 2
3. 4
4. 2
5. 24

DAY 5
1. 35
2. 40
3. yes
4. no
6. rectangle cut into fourths

Final Assessment

1. 16
2. $9
3. 3
4. 14, even
5. 29
6. 41
7. 3+3+3+3 = 12 or 4+4+4 = 12
8. 183
9. 309
10. >
11. 225, 235, 245, 255
12. 40
13. 81
14. 355
15. 395
16. 81
17. 14 cm
18. 4 cm
19. 24 cm
20. 110 m
21. 19 in
22. 41, 52
23. 4:30
24. $2.60
25. 1 dollar 1 quarter 4 pennies
26. 1
27. 8
28. 10
29. 5
30. fourths